Just Inn Time
for Breakfast

A Cookbook from the Michigan
Lake To Lake Bed and Breakfast Association

Tracy & Phyllis Winters

Winters Publishing
P.O. Box 501
Greensburg, Indiana 47240

(812) 663-4948

Cover photograph: Copyright 1992 Stephen J. Pyle
Cover design by Cheryl C. Cigan, Computer & Business
Services of Suttons Bay, Michigan

The information about the inns and the recipes were supplied by the inns themselves. The rate information was current at the time of submission, but is subject to change. Every effort has been made to assure that the book is accurate. Neither the inns, authors, or publisher assume responsibility for any errors, whether typographical or otherwise.

Library of Congress Card Catalog Number 92-62090
ISBN 0-9625329-4-0

Acknowledgements

We would like to thank the Lake To Lake Bed & Breakfast Association for working with us on this project, and all of the innkeepers who took valuable time to select recipes and fill out questionnaires. Special thanks to Lynda Petty and Jan Kerr for their help. It is because of all of their efforts that we were able to make this book a reality.

Preface

Just Inn Time For Breakfast is the culmination of two years of hard work! It was at our State B&B Conference in November, 1990, that the idea of capturing a bit of breakfast table talk was born. As each innkeeper knows, mornings are often filled creating the recipe of successful innkeeping: one helping of history, a bit of baking, cups of cleaning, and a measure of guests binding it all together, and making the recipe work. Each morning the recipe goes together a bit differently, and some mornings the mix is extraordinary! These are the mornings that keep us "cooking", and that we have captured in this book.

The innkeepers on these pages are all members of Lake to Lake Bed & Breakfast Association. Association members are committed to blending warm hospitality and "at home" comfort with the highest standards of cleanliness and safety. . . and making it look easy! Each spring, Lake to Lake produces a directory of all of its members including descriptions, credit card information, seasons of operation, and rates. Copies may be picked up free of charge at member inns or mailed to you for a $3.00 postage and handling fee. We invite you to order your copy by sending a check to Michigan Directory, P.O. Box 428, Saugatuck, MI 49453 or by phoning Travel Directory Books (800) 83-BOOKS, for a Visa/MasterCard order.

The realization of *Just Inn Time For Breakfast* is credited to our many contributers and a few folks without whom the idea would have died on the vine. Special thanks goes to Bob Fuehr, The Innbroker; Sheila McCormack, Innviews; and Joseph Lucido, The Lucido Insurance Agency, for financial support which helped get the ball rolling.

As innkeepers we hope you will enjoy reading our stories, trying our recipes, and using our household hints. And when you need a little break from life as you find it; come see us. After all, you'll be *Just Inn Time For Breakfast!*

CONTENTS

MUFFINS

BLUEBERRY BUTTERMILK MUFFINS

2 1/2 cups all-purpose flour
2 1/2 teaspoons baking powder
1 cup sugar
1/4 teaspoon salt
1 cup buttermilk
2 eggs, beaten
1/4 lb. butter, melted
1 1/2 cups fresh or dry-pack frozen blueberries, rinsed and drained

Sift dry ingredients together into large bowl. Make a well, add buttermilk, eggs, and butter which has been melted and browned slightly. Mix well. Fold in blueberries. Fill well-greased muffin tins half full and bake at 400° for 20 minutes. Serve warm. Makes 12 muffins.

Origin: From Michigan Blueberry Association.

A profusion of petunias edges the walkways, and a distinctive fieldstone fence bounds this picturesque farmstead. "Our big gambrel-roofed barn once housed a registered Ayrshire dairy herd," explain cordial hosts Sue and Bob Chaffin. "Nowadays, our sons grow pickling cucumbers, sugar beets, dry edible beans, corn, wheat and soybeans. We like hosting guests in our turn of the century home, which has original oak woodwork, an open stairway and beamed kitchen. Folks tell us how much they enjoy the peacefulness of our place!" Heirloom quilts and family antiques add comfort for up to six guests in two rooms sharing a bath. Over a country breakfast, you'll enjoy chatting about the area's agriculture and recreational appeal.

To receive more information about CHAFFIN'S BALMORAL FARM B&B write or call: 1245 W. Washington Rd., Ithaca, MI 48847
(517) 875-3410

CINNAMON SOUR CREAM MUFFINS

1 1/2 cups sugar
1 cup butter
5 eggs
1 tablespoon vanilla
2 teaspoons baking powder
1 teaspoon baking soda
4 cups flour
24 oz. sour cream
1 tablespoon cinnamon
1/2 cup sugar
*** Apple, peach or blueberry pie filling (opt.)**

Mix together sugar and butter with wire whisk. Add eggs, vanilla, baking powder, and baking soda. Add flour and sour cream. Mixture will be thick. Spray muffin pan with non-stick cooking spray. Fill half full with batter. Sprinkle cinnamon/sugar mixture on first layer. Fill with remaining batter and top with remaining cinnamon/sugar. * Fruit filling can be added instead of cinnamon/sugar in the middle. Bake at 350° for 25 - 60 minutes. Can also be made in loaf pans instead of muffins. Makes 2 large loaves or 24 muffins.

THE MICHIGAMME LAKE LODGE is on the National and State Register of Historical Sites. Exclusive B&B, situated on the shore of Lake Michigamme atop a bluff overlooking the lake and river. The lodge was built in 1934 for a well-known UP businessman, financier and philanthropist. The lodge is a fine example of the Great Camps that once punctuated the Upper Michigan wilderness. These large lodges received inspiration from the Adirondak style, which emphasized use of natural native materials and a rustic structural simplicity. The lodge has nine rooms, a massive stone fireplace and hand-hewn stairways that lead to twin balconies. There are oak floors, custom made furnishings and a cedar root chandelier. 1700 feet of shoreline for you to enjoy sandy beaches, swimming, fishing, boating, canoeing, hiking and biking trails.

To receive more information about MICHIGAMME LAKE LODGE RESORT B&B write or call: P.O. Box 97, Champion, MI 49814
(906) 339-4400 or (800) 358-0058

HEALTHFUL BRAN MUFFINS

- **2 sticks margarine, melted**
- **2 cups water, warm**
- **3 cups sugar or 2 cups honey**
- **3 teaspoons salt**
- **4 eggs, beaten**
- **1 box All Bran**
- **5 cups flour, unbleached**
- **2 cups quick oatmeal**
- **6 teaspoons baking soda**
- **1 quart buttermilk**

Mix first 8 ingredients. Dissolve soda and buttermilk and add to the already mixed ingredients. Bake in greased muffin tins at 400° for 20 minutes. 2 cups raisins or 2 cups chopped walnuts or pecans may be added for variety. Batter may be stored in refrigerator for up to 3 weeks, using as needed. Makes 5 dozen.

Origin: This recipe originally came from my sister-in-law, but I made so many changes, that I now call it the Kingsley House specialty.

THE KINGSLEY HOUSE is an elegant Queen Anne Victorian inn, built in 1886, and named after the original owner and builder of the house. All guest rooms have private baths, some with jaccuzi suites. We had the distinction to be named "Top 50 Inn in America" by Inn Times and Frommers. Saugatuck and Holland, as well as Lake Michigan with its sandy beaches, are just minutes away. A full breakfast is served each morning on a table set with Royal Doulton china and fine linens. One of our recent guests had lived in the inn when still a child. He came to spend his honeymoon in the room which had belonged to him. He shared precious memories of the past, and left the original architectural drawings of the house as a gift.

To receive more information about THE KINGSLEY HOUSE write or call: 626 West Main St., Fennville, MI 49408 (616) 561-6425

"HEALTHY HEART" MUFFINS

1 cup egg substitute
2 tablespoons sugar
2 teaspoons vanilla
2 cups canned pumpkin
3/4 cup flour
2 teaspoons baking soda
2 teaspoons cinnamon
4 teaspoons pumpkin pie spice
1/2 teaspoon orange peel
1/3 cup dry powdered milk
1/2 cup raisins
1/2 cup shredded carrots
1/2 cup shredded zucchini

Whip egg substitute, sugar, vanilla and canned pumpkin. Stir in flour baking soda, cinnamon, pumpkin pie spice, orange peel, and powdered milk. Add raisins, carrots and zucchini. Pour mixture into muffin pans coated with nonstick spray. Bake at 325° for 20 - 25 minutes or until toothpick comes out clean. Store in refrigerator or freeze. To reheat, microwave on high about 15 seconds. Makes 24 muffins, 70 calories each.

One of the HEART HOUSE INN's previous owners was a heart surgeon. Today, the inn is owned and operated by the sister and brother team of Kelly and Kurt Zurvalec. A majority of our menu items have a healthy heart orientation. All of our fried foods are fried in supreme fry-on, a blend of corn and canola oil, low in saturated fats, with no cholesterol. We cut and drain the fat from our meats, use nonstick commercial cookware and provide nutritional information on our meals. This 8,000 sq. ft. mansion, built during the Civil War, features black walnut beams, lumber, and stained glass, and is furnished with working class furniture from the 1920's - 1940's. The sounds of Roaring 20's Jazz/Glenn Miller Orchestra, etc. are piped into the dining room during lunch and dinner hours.

To receive more information about HEART HOUSE INN write or call:
419 N. Michigan Ave., Saginaw, MI 48602 (517) 753-3145

LEMON POPPY SEED MUFFINS

6 tablespoons butter
6 tablespoons shortening
1 cup sugar
2 eggs
2/3 cup milk
1/3 cup lemon juice
3 cups flour
4 teaspoons baking powder
1 teaspoon salt
1/4 cup poppy seeds
4 teaspoons grated lemon zest

Glaze:
2 cups powdered sugar
1/4 cup lemon juice
1 teaspoon vanilla

Preheat oven to 350°. Put paper liners in muffin cups. Cream together butter, shortening, and sugar. Beat in eggs, milk, and lemon juice. In separate bowl, combine flour, baking powder, and salt. Add to creamed mixture a little at a time. Stir in poppy seeds and lemon zest. Fill muffin cups 2/3 full. Bake 25 minutes. Glaze: Mix all ingredients. Drizzle over slightly cooled muffins. Makes 12 muffins.

Built in 1898 by Egbert Ferris, THE VICTORIANA has the only gazebo in Traverse City. An artesian well, used during typhoid epidemics, is still flowing at the rear of the house. A two-story carriage house complements the back yard, while an Indian trail marker tree graces the front yard. This classy Victorian home with tiled fireplaces, oak staircase and gingerbread trim is furnished with an eclectic mix of selected antiques, Victorian pieces and traditional furniture. Guest rooms offer an individual style. Soon after innkeepers Flo and Bob Schermerhorn opened the inn, a caller made a reservation and asked for the room with an arch in the sitting area. When asked how she knew that particular room, she answered, "I grew up in that house and it was my room." Her stay was a trip down memory lane and a homecoming.

To receive more information about THE VICTORIANA 1898 write or call: 622 Washington Street, Traverse City, MI 49684
(616) 929-1009

MICHIGAN DRIED CHERRY MUFFINS

1/2 cup dried cherries and orange juice to cover
1 egg
1/2 cup milk
1/4 cup salad oil
1 1/2 cups flour
1/2 cup sugar
2 teaspoons baking powder
1/2 teaspoon salt

Topping:
1/2 cup finely chopped nuts
1/2 cup brown sugar

Soak dried cherries in orange juice overnight (or speed up process by microwaving on low for 2 minutes and allow them to cool). Mix together egg, milk, oil, and drained cherries. Mix together dry ingredients in separate bowl. Combine dry ingredients with wet. Drop into greased mini muffin tins. Mix nuts and brown sugar together. Top muffins. Bake at 400° for 8 - 10 minutes. Makes 4 dozen mini muffins.

THE CLOGHAUN, built in 1884, is on Mackinac Island's historic Market Street. The home was built by Bridgett and Thomas Donnelly to house their large Irish family. It is still owned and operated by their descendants. Mackinac Island is a favorite place for weddings and honeymoons. One night an overly romantic honeymoon couple decided to bathe together, causing a minor flood in the library below their room. This was an unusual event. More often guests may be called upon to witness weddings of those being married in the home's library.

To receive more information about CLOGHAUN write or call:
P.O.Box 203 (Market St.), Mackinac Island, MI 49757
(906) 847-3885 or (313) 331-7110 (winter)

ORANGE PECAN MUFFINS

1/2 cup butter
1 cup sugar
2 eggs
2 cups flour
1 teaspoon baking powder
1/2 teaspoon salt
1 cup buttermilk
Juice & rind of one orange, divided use
1 cup chopped nuts
1/3 cup sugar

Preheat oven to 375°. Cream butter and sugar. Beat in eggs one at a time. Sift together flour, baking powder, and salt. Add to creamed butter and sugar. Stir in buttermilk, orange rind, and pecans. Turn into greased muffin tin and bake 20 minutes. Combine orange juice and 1/3 cup sugar and heat to boiling. Pour over baked muffins. Makes 12 muffins.

The summer of 1991 looked to be a very prosperous one, the calendar was filling up very nicely. Then the cancellations began! It was frightening. Early in August, as I served a lone guest breakfast, the phone rang with the caller prefacing her inquiry with "I have reservations with you for August 30. . ." I felt that fear of another cancellation coming. The caller continued with "We've decided to get married while we are there. Can you please give me the name of a minister? And maybe you can help find a photographer, a hairdresser and some flowers?" It seems this couple became engaged about 15 years ago in Lithuania while she was visiting from the U.S. Her letters were destroyed and phone calls were diverted. Each married another and divorced. Friends reunited them, and we had a beautiful ceremony, with a happy bride and groom, and champagne on our porch afterwards!

To receive more information about BELLAIRE BED & BREAKFAST,
write or call: 212 Park St., Bellaire, MI 49615
(616) 533-6077 or (800) 545-0780

SUNSHINE MUFFINS

1 1/2 cups sugar
1/2 cup oil
1 egg, beaten
2 teaspoons grated lemon peel
2 teaspoons grated orange peel
1/2 cup orange juice
Juice of one lemon
2 1/2 cups all-purpose flour
1 teaspoon baking powder
1 teaspoon baking soda
1/2 teaspoon salt

Cream together sugar and oil in large bowl. Add egg, lemon peel, orange peel, orange juice and lemon juice. In separate bowl, combine flour, baking powder, baking soda, and salt. Add to creamed mixture and stir until just blended. Bake in greased muffin tins in 350° oven for 30 minutes. Makes 1 1/2 dozen muffins.

Origin: My daughter Tami and I decided that even though we live in Michigan, it would be fun to serve our guests a taste of our home state, the Sunshine State. This is the recipe we created.

THE SIDE PORCH, an Italianate style home was built in 1870. Around the turn of the century the house was occupied by a Mr. Case who manufactured a patent medicine, involving wax melted onto cloth used as a plaster, thus earning it's inventor the nickname of "Sticking Salve Case." All of our guests at THE SIDE PORCH have been wonderful and very special, and our very first guests have a unique way of returning each year - with each visit they purchase a gift certificate to ensure their return the next year!!

To receive more information about THE SIDE PORCH B&B write or call: 120 College Street, Holly, MI 48442 (313) 634-0740

WILD BLACKBERRY MUFFINS

1 cup rolled oats
1 cup buttermilk
1/4 cup canola oil
1/4 cup honey
1 egg
1 cup whole wheat flour
1 teaspoon baking powder
1/2 teaspoon salt
1/2 teaspoon baking soda
1 cup wild blackberries (fresh or frozen)

Soak oats in buttermilk overnight. Mix in oil, honey and egg. Add flour to which baking powder, salt and soda have been added. Stir in blackberries. Spray muffin tins with Pam. Fill 2/3 full, and bake at 400° for 20 - 25 minutes. Makes 12 muffins.

Our favorite guests are those that come time after time because they share our love for our ideal setting and the simple elegance that surrounds them. BEAR RIVER VALLEY is in the country between lakes and streams, woodlands, and little towns and villages. Being seasoned outdoor enthusiasts, we want to offer our guests a mixture of fun, luxury, serenity, comfort, wilderness experience, and civilization. Before we send them off exploring our beautiful area, we fortify them with a nutritious gourmet breakfast. Then, at the end of their day, we invite them to enjoy an authentic Finnish sauna bath or just relax peacefully in front of a crackling fire or on one of our decks or porches. They report this is what they return for again and again.

To receive more information about BEAR RIVER VALLEY B&B write or call: 03636 Bear River Rd., Petoskey, MI 49770 (616) 348-2046

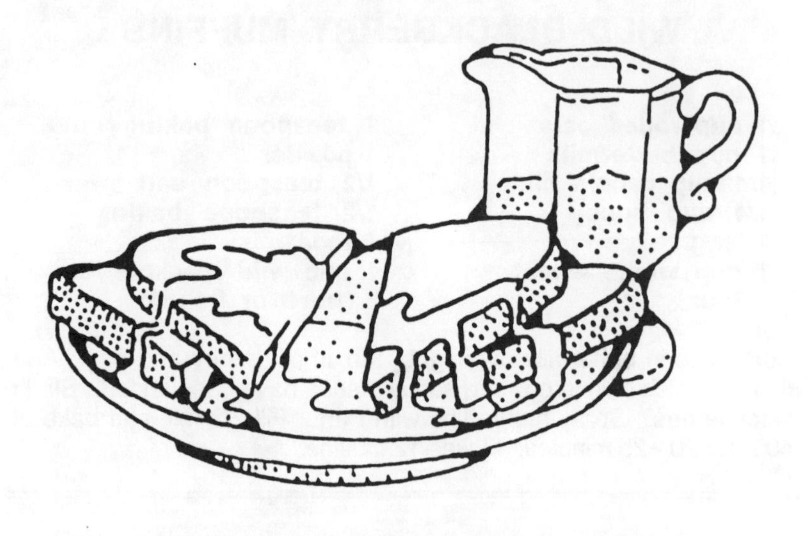

FRENCH TOAST, PANCAKES & WAFFLES

BAKED FRENCH BREAD

6 large eggs
1 1/2 cups milk
1 cup light cream or half & half
1 1/4 teaspoons vanilla
1/4 teaspoon cinnamon
1/4 teaspoon nutmeg
1 loaf French bread (cut 1" thick diagonally)
1/4 cup softened butter
1/2 cup firmly packed light brown sugar
1/2 cup chopped walnuts (opt.)
1 tablespoon light corn syrup

Butter a large baking dish. In medium bowl combine eggs, milk, cream, vanilla, cinnamon, and nutmeg. Place bread in baking dish in single layer with sides touching. Pour entire mixture over bread, cover, and refrigerate overnight. Preheat oven to 350°. In small bowl combine butter, brown sugar, walnuts and corn syrup. Spread evenly over bread. Bake 40 minutes or until puffed and golden. Serves 6 - 8.

Return to yesteryear. 1880's Queen Anne Victorian decorated with family and area antiques, located in the Irish Hills area 15 minutes from 54 lakes. Close to antiquing, shopping, hiking, biking, county and state parks, swimming and golfing. Special care is what we offer our guests. When an area resident asked us to reserve a room for his 81 year old mother, we were concerned about the stairs, and a possible special breakfast diet. When she arrived, we discovered she had back-packed England alone at age 65.

To receive more information about CHICAGO STREET INN write or call: 219 Chicago St., Brooklyn, MI 49230 (517) 592-3888

BUTTERMILK CINNAMON WAFFLES WITH DRIED CHERRIES

6 extra large eggs
2 tablespoons sugar
2 1/2 cups buttermilk
1/2 cup vegetable oil
1 tablespoon vanilla
1/2 cup dried cherries
2 cups flour
1 1/3 cups wheat flour
1 tablespoon baking powder
1 1/2 teaspoons baking soda
1 heaping tablespoon cinnamon

Soak dried cherries in liquid for 15 minutes before mixing with ingredients. Mix first six ingredients, including cherries. Mix dry ingredients together and add to the liquid ingredients. Mix. This can be frozen. Cook according to manufacturer's direction in waffle iron. Makes 6 - 8 servings.

A place where relaxing days are spent with wildlife right outside your doorstep and delightful, country comforts are experienced within. To start your day, a plentiful breakfast prepared with products indigenous to Leelanau County is served each morning. Take a ferry ride to South Manitou Island and the Grand Traverse Lighthouse Museum, tour wineries, or stroll the streets of a 200 year old fishing village, with galleries, antiques and novelty nooks for browsing. A four-season inn, located in the heart of cherry country. A first-time California visitor to Michigan and the Leelanau Peninsula was in awe, and asked if all of our lakes were fresh water.

To receive more information about MANITOU MANOR B&B write or call: P.O. Box 864, Leland, MI 49654 (616) 256-7712

COTTAGE CHEESE BLENDER PANCAKES

1 cup cottage cheese
6 eggs
1/2 cup flour
1/4 teaspoon salt
1/4 cup vegetable oil
1/4 cup milk
1/2 teaspoon vanilla
Raspberry Sauce:
1 cup seedless raspberry jam
1 cup honey
1 cup margarine

Put all pancake ingredients into blender and blend thoroughly. Refrigerate at least 12 hours. Remove from refrigerator, stir only once. Pour pancakes onto hot griddle. When bubbles show through, flip and fry other side. Do not overbrown. Roll up on end of wooden spoon. Dust with powdered sugar and serve with Raspberry or Cherry Sauce. Boil jam, honey and margarine. Stir and cool. Serve warm. Refrigerate leftover sauce. Makes 6 servings.

Dorothy and Percy Cump have owned what is now CHERRY KNOLL FARM B&B since 1968. This circa 1865 farmhouse was sorely neglected. When the Cumps retired in 1988 and moved to Traverse City, renovations began. After 6 months, they decided to open a B&B which was their way of keeping in touch with people. What a perfect choice! Recently an exhausted couple arrived. They had worked all day, taken their girls to their grandparents home, and driven for 3 hours. They were upstairs only a few minutes when they came back downstairs, looking quite sheepish, and asked for toothbrushes, etc. Seemed they had brought the wrong suitcase and only had "little people" clothes, blankets, and teddy bears.

To receive more information about CHERRY KNOLL FARM B&B write or call: 2856 Hammond Road East, Traverse City, MI 49684 (616) 947-9806

CREPES

3 eggs, beaten
1/2 cup half & half
1/2 cup flour

Filling:
4 oz. cream cheese, softened
1/2 cup sour cream
2 tablespoons sugar
1/2 teaspoon almond extract

Beat eggs, add half & half. Beat well. Add flour slowly. Beat with a whisk. Let stand about 5 minutes before cooking. Pour about 1/4 cup batter onto lightly buttered hot 10" skillet. Tilt pan to spread evenly. Cook until lightly browned, turn and cook other side. Spread with 1 tablespoon filling and roll up. Serve with fresh fruit. Makes 10 crepes.

Denny and Martie Lorenz, the proprietors of THE HURON HOUSE BED & BREAKFAST, go out of their way to make their guests feel at home. The guests come back time after time to enjoy the delicious breakfasts, the spectacular sunrises, the long walks on the beautiful sandy beach, the relaxing atmosphere, and the hot tub under the stars. Whatever your preference, friendly and warm hospitality awaits you!

To receive more information about HURON HOUSE B&B write or call:
3124 N. U.S. 23, Oscoda, MI 48750 (517) 739-9255

GERMAN PUFF PANCAKE

1/3 cup butter
5 eggs
1 1/4 cups flour
1 1/4 cups milk
1/2 lb. bacon, fried crisply & crumbled
1/2 cup Swiss cheese

Preheat oven to 425°. Place butter in 8" iron skillet and put in oven to melt. In medium bowl beat eggs with beater. Add flour and milk and beat until smooth. Do not overbeat. Pour batter into hot buttered skillet and bake for 20 - 25 minutes. At the last 5 minutes, remove from oven and add bacon and cheese on top. Return to oven and finish baking. Will be puffed and golden. Loosen with a knife and cut into wedges. Serve hot. Makes 4 - 6 servings.

CENTENNIAL BED & BREAKFAST occupies the Philip L. Wixson house, built in 1879 and now on the Michigan State Historical Register. The original clapboard siding and large windows provide an historic and romantic setting for this modern day B&B. Guests enjoy the traditional, antique furnishings, comfortable queen size beds, spacious and elegant lawns and gardens, and the sumptuous breakfasts served family style on fine china and silver. Our guests return again and again to CENTENNIAL, located on Lake Huron, and to their hosts, who do their best to make guests feel so welcome and special.

To receive more information about CENTENNIAL B&B write or call:
5774 Main St., Lexington, MI 48450 (313) 359-8762

LAATZ PANCAKES (GERMAN)

3/4 cup flour
Pinch of salt
3 large eggs
1/2 cup milk
1/2 cup melted butter
1 tablespoon lemon juice
Cinnamon sugar mixture
Fresh fruit, hot apple-sauce, blueberries, (opt.) & maple syrup

Heat oven to 400°. Place your best cast iron skillet or ovenproof fry pan in oven to heat. Cover bottom of pan with a little oil or spray with Pam. Mix flour and salt. Mix eggs and milk in blender. Mix liquid with dry ingredients. Pour into hot skillet and bake approximately 20 minutes. Remove from oven. Pancake will fall. Drizzle melted butter and lemon juice over pancake. Sprinkle with cinnamon-sugar. Cut into wedges. Serve with fruit, applesauce, blueberries, and maple syrup. Makes 4 servings.

Origin: From my father.

GORTON HOUSE is located in the heart of the Sunrise Side of Michigan. Travelers arrive in Lewiston (Fun Country, USA) from all across the country. As the gentleman from California stated, "A little golf - a little snow - a lot of fun." Or, as the young couple from 300 miles south noted, "This is like coming home to Mom's." THE GORTON HOUSE is "a place like home . . . away from home!" A fantastic breakfast is served each morning on the porch which affords a splendid view of Little Wolf Lake. Guests can watch the fish rise from the water or catch a glimpse of the spectacular loon as he dives beneath the lake. "Words cannot describe. . ." and "I don't wanna' go" are frequently echoed from the guests.

To receive more information about GORTON HOUSE write or call:
14176 Ellen Dr., Livonia, MI 48514 (mailing address)
(313) 261-5347 or (517) 786-2764 (Lewiston, MI 49756)

PUFF PANCAKES

3 large eggs
1/2 cup milk
1/2 cup all-purpose flour
Pinch of cinnamon
1/4 teaspoon granulated sugar
Pinch of salt
1 tablespoon unsalted butter

Sliced Granny Smith apples, to taste
1/4 cup unsalted butter
1/2 cup granulated sugar
Dash of cinnamon
Fresh lemon juice

Powdered sugar

Whisk eggs with milk. Whisk in flour, pinch of cinnamon, 1/4 teaspoon sugar, and a pinch of salt. Combine well. Divide 1 tablespoon butter among 3 large non-stick muffin cups, melt butter in moderate oven. Rotate pan to coat sides of cups. Divide batter among 3 cups. Bake at 425° for 15 minutes. Meanwhile, sauté apples in 1/4 cup butter with 1/2 cup sugar, dash of cinnamon and lemon juice to taste. Spoon sauce over pancakes on serving plate, and dust with powdered sugar. Makes 3 large servings.

BROCKWAY HOUSE, an historic treasure for generations is an enchanting and elegant B&B where a warm hearth and personal family attention are part of the daily menu. The atmosphere draws you back to 1864, the year the home was built by Able Brockway, lumber baron and family man. Starting on the roof, BROCKWAY HOUSE has been completely restored and redecorated, using a collection of the Zuehlke's primitive antiques. One of the recent guests commented, "Everything is antique except the mattresses, we had a peaceful night's rest in an historic setting." The innkeepers love to cook and prepare full gourmet breakfasts each morning. Our guests decide what time is best for them and we willingly pamper them.

To receive more information about BROCKWAY HOUSE B&B write or call: 1631 Brockway, Saginaw, MI 48602 (517) 792-0746

SURPRISE FRENCH TOAST

8 slices very thinly sliced Pepperidge Farm white bread
4 oz. light soft cream cheese
1/2 cup chopped pecans or English walnuts
2 eggs
1/4 cup milk
1/4 teaspoon salt
Cinnamon (opt.)

Cream together cream cheese and chopped nuts. Make four sandwiches from the bread, and spread with this filling. Whisk together eggs, milk, salt, and cinnamon. Dip each sandwich in the egg mixture, and brown both sides on a preheated hot griddle. Serve with your favorite syrup. Makes 4 - 1 sandwich servings.

The 1893 HEALD-LEAR HOUSE has walls and floors filled with early Grand Rapids history -- if only those walls could talk! Relatives of former owners have visited with Dorothy and Murray Stout, current hosts, told of grand entertaining that took over the house in the past -- and even shown them the "secret room", which the Stouts had not found up to that point. From whatever walk of life, U.S. Senator, foreign business person, newlywed, traveller, or guest who has become friend, guests seem to most enjoy breakfast in the solarium, while viewing the colorful garden and listening to the cheerful splash of the water in the marble fountain.

To receive more information about HEALD-LEAR HOUSE write or call: 455 College Ave. S.E., Grand Rapids, MI 49503
(616) 451-4849

WATER STREET INN PANCAKES

2 cups rolled oats
2 cups buttermilk
2 eggs, lightly beaten
1/4 cup butter, melted (1/2 stick)
1/2 cup all-purpose flour
2 tablespoons sugar
1 teaspoon baking powder
1 teaspoon baking soda
1/2 teaspoon cinnamon
1/4 teaspoon salt

Combine the oats and buttermilk in bowl and stir to blend. Cover and refrigerate overnight. Next morning add beaten eggs and melted butter, and stir. Mix dry ingredients in small bowl (pre-measure the night before), and add to batter. Use 1/4 cup batter for each pancake. Cook on hot griddle and serve with maple syrup. Makes 1 1/2 dozen pancakes.

A Victorian welcome awaits you at THE WATER STREET INN BED & BREAKFAST. This restored Queen Anne home is located in one of the oldest cities in the U.S., just 1 1/2 blocks from the Soo Locks. Our large parlor and library invite you to step back in time and relax in the manner of bygone days. Many tranquil hours are spent on the spacious wraparound porch and gazebo watching the slowly passing freighters. We are rumored to have a friendly ghost because of the hastily invented story of a young tour guide whose group of tourists persisted in looking at our inn, instead of the historical markers on the opposite side of the street.

To receive more information about THE WATER STREET INN write or call: 140 Water St., Sault Ste. Marie, MI 49783
906) 632-1900 or (800) 236-1904

EGG, MEAT & CHEESE DISHES

BAKED EGG DISH

1 pkg. crescent rolls
2 cups shredded Monterey Jack cheese
4 eggs
3/4 cup milk
1/4 cup chopped pepper
1/4 teaspoon oregano
Salt & pepper to taste

Grease 9" x 12" pan. Pat crescent rolls into pan, going up the sides. Mix remaining ingredients. Pour into crust. Bake for half an hour at 375° to 400°. Makes 4 servings.

We had a group of home economists who came here after a conference in Lansing and stayed two days. One lady remarked on the toilet paper. She said it was the most marvelous toilet paper. She said she couldn't get that particular brand where she lived. After they left, Linda, the housekeeper, came down from doing the beds and the bathrooms and said, "You're not going to believe this, but all the toilet paper is gone. **Every** roll from **every** bathroom!"

To receive more information about CIDER HOUSE B&B write or call:
5515 Barney Road, Traverse City, MI 49684 (616) 947-2833

BREAKFAST CASSEROLE

2 1/2 cups herbed croutons
1 lb. bulk sausage, cooked & drained
2 cups grated sharp Cheddar cheese
1 small can mushroom pieces
6 eggs, well-beaten
1 1/4 cups milk
1/2 teaspoon salt
1/2 teaspoon garlic salt
1/2 cup French onion chip dip
1 can mushroom soup

Grease 9" x 13" dish. Layer croutons, sauage, cheese, and mushrooms. Beat eggs and add milk, salt, garlic salt, chip dip, and soup. Pour over mixture in dish. Bake in preheated oven of 300° for 1 1/2 hours. Makes 6 generous servings.

A couple who stayed at our Bed and Breakfast recently were the guest soloists with our city's symphony orchestra. They had never stayed at a Bed and Breakfast, and enjoyed the special treatment, including fresh flowers, a snack tray, and Godiva chocolates which they found in their room. That evening, when they began dressing for the concert, the husband came down looking rather pale, and said that his wife had forgotten to pack his tuxedo shirt! We were quick to loan him one of my husband's shirts, and when he appeared on stage that evening, we were especially delighted not only in his performance, but to know that my husband's shirt had saved the day; another service which he could not have gotten at a hotel.

To receive more information about SUMMIT PLACE B&B write or call:
1682 W. Kimmel Rd., Jackson, MI 49201 (517) 787-0468

CORNED BEEF PIE

2 - 15 oz. cans corned beef hash
1 cup shredded cheese (Swiss, Cheddar, or mixture)
1 cup chopped celery
1/4 cup chopped onion
4 eggs, beaten
1/2 cup Bisquick
1 cup milk

Combine hash and one egg. Press lightly into greased 9 1/2" pie plate to form crust. Mix remaining eggs and Bisquick until smooth, blend in milk, pour onto crust. Bake at 375° for 35 - 40 minutes, or until center is firm. Let stand 5 minutes before cutting. Serves 6 - 8.

One of the interesting challenges of innkeeping is making the first time "B&B-er" relax and feel "at home". Several years ago, a young woman came to the door, and with great embarrassment said, "My husband won't get out of the car! He's afraid he has to share his toothbrush!" I was just preparing afternoon aperitifs, so I poured a large glassful of Leelanau's finest wine, and sent it to him in the car. By the end of their 3-day visit, along with swims on Grand Traverse Bay, breakfast popovers, Eggs Benedict, and the daily social afternoon repast, Dan was a committed soul! Now, Lou Ann and Dan visit several times a year. He enjoys playing "host" whenever he is in residence.

To receive more information about NORTH SHORE INN write or call:
12271 N. Northport Point Rd., Northport, MI 49670
(616) 386-7111

DILLED EGGS

12 eggs, beaten
1 - 2 teaspoons dried dill weed
Salt to taste
Freshly ground pepper
1/4 - 1/2 teaspoon granulated garlic (use less garlic powder)
Water for scrambling

Beat eggs and add seasonings and water. Beat well. Scramble in hot skillet. Serve eggs with bacon or ham. Makes 6 servings.

Origin: A family recipe.

THE HOMESTEAD is the oldest B&B (both in 8 plus years of operation as a B&B and in terms of when it was built, 1851) in the Ann Arbor - Ypsilanti area. We find that more often than not, guests gathered around the breakfast table find that they have a great deal in common: interests, areas of work, geographic location, or some other common theme. This happens so consistently that it no longer surprises us. During our first year of operation, 4 couples, all from the Detroit area, sat at the breakfast table. Although none of them had met before, they found that they actually lived in the same neighborhood, all within 1/8 mile from each other. They became such good friends as a result of this chance encounter, that they have returned as a group every year since that first year.

To receive more information about THE HOMESTEAD B&B write or call: 9279 Macon Rd., Saline, MI 49236 (313) 429-9625

EGG BAKE

6 eggs, beaten
1 cup cottage cheese, large curd
1 bunch green onions, chopped, with tops
1 pkg. dried beef, cut up
Salt & pepper to taste
Topping: 1/2 cup sharp grated Cheddar cheese

Beat eggs, mix with cottage cheese, onions, and dried beef, adding salt and pepper to taste. Bake in individual dishes or in a 9" x 9" glass baking dish. Top with grated cheese. Bake at 350° for 30 minutes. Serve immediately. May be made the night before. Makes 4 servings.

In 1874, wealthy land developer John Wenham built this home which was occupied by three generations of his family before becoming a multi-family dwelling in 1940. The home was purchased in 1986 and restoration began, returning it to single family elegance. The new B&B opened in 1987. Soon after, an elderly man appeared at the door and inquired about the house. He began by relating the story that his wife and her sister were born in this house, and he wanted to surprise them with a reservation. A week later, the sisters were sipping wine in the parlor while telling stories and sharing old photographs of the Wenham's home. These candid family photos and stories are part of what is shared with our guests.

To receive more information about FOUNTAIN HILL B&B write or call:
222 Fountain N.E., Grand Rapids, MI 49503 (616) 458-6621

GARDEN CRUSTLESS QUICHE

- 5 eggs
- 1/4 cup flour
- 1/2 teaspoon baking powder
- 1/8 teaspoon salt
- 1 cup cottage cheese
- 1/2 lb. Monterey Jack cheese, shredded
- 4 tablespoons butter
- 1 onion, peeled & chopped
- 4 green onions, sliced thinly
- 2 green zucchini, sliced
- 2 yellow squash, sliced
- 1/2 cup parsley, chopped
- 3 tomatoes, sliced thinly

Whip eggs until fluffy and set aside. In another bowl mix dry ingredients, stir in cottage cheese. Mix together with eggs and half of the Monterey Jack cheese. Sauté onion in butter until softened. Add to egg mixture along with green onions, zucchini, yellow squash, and parsley. Pour into a 10" pie plate or quiche dish. Top with remaining Monterey Jack cheese and then with tomato slices. Bake at 400° for 10 minutes, reduce to 350° and continue to bake 25 - 30 minutes, or until top is lightly browned. Cool slightly and serve.

HALL HOUSE stands at the entrance to Kalamazoo's finest historic neighborhood, 5 blocks west of the city & 1 block north of Kalamazoo College. As the new owners of HALL HOUSE we find it particularly gratifying to hear from guests who find great pleasure in the "little things" we do. Their praise of our efforts and their obvious joy at feeling "pampered" gives us good feelings too. Innkeeping is a very special way to make a difference. . . and FUN! Give us a call and come visit us! Quality personal service is our HALLmark. . . guaranteed!

To receive more information about HALL HOUSE write or call:
106 Thompson St., Kalamazoo, MI 49006 (616) 343-2500

"GOOD MORNING" SAUSAGE BALLS

1 lb. good quality sausage
1 cup fresh bread crumbs
1 egg
2 teaspoons soy sauce
1/2 cup chopped pecans
2 teaspoons cornstarch

Mix ingredients together. Roll into small balls. Pan fry or bake well. Serve with warm applesauce.

CANDLELIGHT COTTAGE hosts many talented and exciting guests, some even of renown. The candlelight from every window beckons visitors from nearby Alma College. The charming English decor and bountiful breakfast please all who have stayed. A recent visitor, author, and lecturer wrote, "Like my artists, your creation of an environment inspires and comforts." Every year at Highland Festival time an English-born actress and family return and delight guests and innkeepers Yvonne and Ron Wolfgang with English plays at teatime. Come and enjoy the warm and traditional atmosphere.

To receive more information about CANDLELIGHT COTTAGE, write or call: 910 Vassar St., Alma, MI 48801 (517) 463-3961

HAM QUICHE

- Pastry for 9" pie plate
- 4 eggs, beaten
- 1/2 - 3/4 cup milk
- 1/4 teaspoon pepper
- 1/4 teaspoon baking powder
- 1 1/2 cups ground cooked ham
- 1 cup shredded Swiss or Cheddar cheese
- 1/4 cup chopped green pepper and 1/4 cup chopped onion (opt.)

Line a 9" quiche pan with pastry, and trim off excess around edge. Place buttered aluminum foil, buttered side down, over pastry, gently press in. Cover foil with a layer of dried peas or beans. Bake at 400° for 10 minutes. Remove foil and peas. Prick shell and bake 3 - 5 additional minutes. Cool. Combine eggs, milk, pepper, and baking powder. Beat well. Stir in remainder of ingredients and spoon into shell. Bake at 425° for 25 - 30 minutes. Makes 4 - 6 servings.

This brick farmhouse stands as it was originally built in 1880 for Barney McGee, who owned 1,000 acres in this lush Irish Catholic farming community. Innkeepers Bill and Ardie Barber have enjoyed a wide variety of guests since opening the HOMESTEAD as a B&B in 1988. Bill has filled the big barn with most every farm animal for the guests to pet. Ardie had newlyweds helping her with the chores and milking the goat one morning - their option.

To receive more information about McGEE HOMESTEAD write or call: 2534 Alden Nash N.E., Lowell, MI 49331 (616) 897-8142

HAVARTI EGGS

1 teaspoon butter, melted
1 tablespoon cream
2 eggs
Salt & pepper to taste
Grated Havarti cheese

Butter a 3 1/2 oz. ramekin or custard dish. Add cream. Gently crack eggs into the ramekin. Season with salt and pepper. Sprinkle Havarti cheese on top. Bake in preheated 425° oven for 8 - 10 minutes, or until the white is firm and the center is still soft. Makes 1 serving.

Five years ago my husband and I bought this 100 year old farmhouse. We didn't know much about the house, other than the fact that for many years it served as a dairy farm. One year ago, I took an art class, and became good friends with one of the other students. Ila Mae Burger, who was delightful, full of energy, and 85, soon discovered that her daddy had built our house. We invited her to come and have dinner with us, and spent the next four hours totally captured by her wonderful stories. She also gave us many great pictures of her family and farm. The pictures have all been placed in a photo album with a story for each picture. It was a special day in my life when I met "Ila Mae Burger."

To receive more information about MAPLEWOOD B&B write or call:
15945 Wood Rd., Lansing, MI 48906 (517) 372-7775

ITALIAN STRATA

3 cloves of garlic, minced
1 small onion, diced
2 tablespoons olive oil
3 medium tomatoes, peeled & chopped
1 small zucchini, diced
1/2 cup mushrooms, sliced
Salt & pepper to taste
Clump each of fresh basil & oregano (or Italian seasoning)
6 slices bread
Margarine for bread
9 eggs
2/3 cup milk
6 oz. mozzarella cheese, shredded
1/8 cup Parmesan cheese, grated

Sauté garlic and onion in olive oil. Add tomatoes, zucchini, mushrooms, and seasonings and cook until tender. Set aside. Spread bread slices with margarine and place face down in baking dish (8" x 11"). Beat eggs with milk. Pour egg mixture and vegetable mixture on top of bread. Top with cheeses. Cover and refrigerate overnight. Bake uncovered at 350° for 45 - 55 minutes or until lightly browned and puffy. Serves 8 - 10.

THE EASTERLY INN was built in 1906 as a result of the great lumber era. Much of the woodwork, still in its original condition, was milled just two blocks away. The house has kept its elegant Victorian charm with the addition of handprinted wallpapers and fine antiques. Romance seems to flourish at THE EASTERLY INN, as we have been the setting for three engagements. We are centrally located in northwest Michigan's resort area offering a wide variety of activities and entertainment.

To receive more information about EASTERLY INN write or call:
P.O. Box 366, 209 Esterly, East Jordan, MI 49727 (616) 536-3434

MORNING PIZZA

- 1/4 cup milk
- 5 eggs
- 1 pkg. pizza crust mix
- 1 lb. sausage, cooked & drained
- 2 cups frozen hash browns
- 1/4 cup Parmesan cheese
- 1 1/2 cups shredded cheese (a variety may be used if desired)
- Mushrooms, peppers, etc. (opt.)
- Picante sauce

Add milk to eggs and scramble in skillet. Prepare pizza dough as directed on package, and pat into 13" greased pizza pan. Spread crumbled sausage on dough. Cover with hash browns, Parmesan cheese, scrambled eggs, and shredded cheese, in that order. Bake at 375° for 25 - 30 minutes. Serve with picante sauce. Excellent recipe. Makes 8 or more servings.

A student attending one of the local colleges wanted to get away from it all and stayed with us. "It's like a visit back home," she stated. She asked if we would take small groups of college students for overnight spiritual retreats. Since then, we have a guest book full of college students who have been treated to a short visit to "home", with home cooking, friendly smiles and lots of hugs!

To receive more information about BLUE COUNTRY B&B, write or call: 1415 Holton Rd., Muskegon, MI 49445 (616) 744-2555

OMENA SHORES CREAMED EGGS

8 strips bacon, cooked crisply & crumbled
1 large onion, sliced
1 can cream of mushroom soup
1 can Cheddar cheese soup
3/4 soup can milk
8 hard boiled eggs, sliced
4 English muffins, split & toasted

Cook bacon until crisp and crumble. Reserve 3 tablespoons bacon drippings. Sauté sliced onion in bacon drippings until wilted. Add mushroom and cheese soups, and milk, stirring until smooth. Heat gently. Add sliced eggs, and stir carefully. Toast English muffins and serve egg mixture on top. Sprinkle crumbled bacon over all. Makes 4 servings.

Origin: My original creation!

Mary Helen Phillips, former innkeeper of Omena Shores B&B, is currently a member of the Lake to Lake Bed & Breakfast Association Board of Review.

POTATO/SAUSAGE CASSEROLE

- **32 oz. pkg. frozen hash browns (thawed)**
- **1 pkg. brown & serve sausage, smokey links, or smoked sausage, cut into bite-sized pieces**
- **1/2 cup melted margarine**
- **1 teaspoon salt**
- **1/8 teaspoon pepper**
- **1 can cream of celery soup**
- **1 soup can warm water**
- **3 1/2 oz. can Durkee onion rings**
- **1 cup Parmesan cheese**

Mix together potatoes, sausage, margarine, salt, and pepper. In separate bowl mix together soup and 1 can warm water. Add 3/4 of soup mixture to other ingredients and blend. Place in 9" x 13" pan (sprayed with Pam) or several smaller bowls (ramekins). Pour remainder of soup across top. On top of soup spread onion rings and Parmesan cheese. Bake at 350° about 30 minutes (until bubbly). Serve hot. This can be refrigerated or frozen until the day it's needed. Can also be rewarmed in microwave. Makes 10 - 12 servings.

Origin: A friend created this recipe to eliminate cheese and eggs from the ingredients for a low cholesterol dish.

The most common comment we get from our guests is "It really IS big!" Our brochure cover has a drawing of our home and it is described as a 3-story, 30 room, 10,000+ square foot Dutch Colonial with Queen Anne influences which was completed in 1894. A highlight is eating in our formal turret dining room by the fire (when it's chilly), at a table set with antique china. We are always pleased to have our guests enjoy the original features in our home - imported wallcoverings from Italy and Paris, imported English oak and black birch woodwork, lead glass windows, light fixtures, and carved wood.

To receive more information about SARAVILLA B&B write or call:
633 N. State St., Alma, MI 48801 (517) 463-4078

SAUSAGE CREPES

Filling:
I lb. bulk sausage, browned & drained
1/4 cup chopped onion
1/2 cup shredded processed cheese
3 oz. cream cheese
1/4 teaspoon dried marjoram

Sauce:
1/2 cup dairy sour cream
1/4 cup butter

Basic crepe recipe of your choice

Cook sausage with onion until lightly browned. Drain. Add shredded cheese, cream cheese and marjoram. Stir. Place about 2 tablespoons filling in middle of crepe and roll up. Place in 11 3/4" x 7 1/2" x 1 3/4" pan (those measurements always kill me - find a funky pan and bake). Cover pan, and chill, a day ahead is fine. Bake covered in 375° oven for 15 minutes, then uncovered until slightly browned. Heat sour cream and butter carefully until warm. Spoon over crepes and serve. Makes 12 crepes.

Origin: This is our most requested recipe, from my Minnesota friend.

TORCH LAKE BED & BREAKFAST sits high on a hill overlooking magnificent Torch Lake. This 1895 Painted Victorian Lady, in architectural jargon, a carpenter gothic, is gently referred to by the locals as the pink gingerbread house. I love that - it fits us and Alden. Our B&B was built by the Main family. He wanted to stand on his front porch and see if his hotel, just down the road a bit, was running smoothly. The first year we began, a pleasant elderly lady stayed with us. In the morning, I asked her what brought her to Alden. Her eyes lit up, and she said, "Well, you see, my grandfather built this house, and I thought it would be a tribute to his memory. You've made me happy by restoring it." And we were happy she came.

To receive more information about TORCH LAKE B&B, write or call:
P.O. Box 165 or 10601 Coy St., Alden, MI 49612 (616) 331-6424

SPICY EGGS

1 dozen hard-boiled eggs
1/2 cup mayonnaise
3 tablespoons spicy mustard
6 drops Tabasco sauce
1/4 cup lemon juice
Pepper to taste
3 cups medium white sauce
8 drops Tabasco sauce
2 teaspoons Worcestershire sauce
1 1/2 pkgs. chipped beef
8 oz. fresh Parmesan cheese

Butter 9" x 13" casserole. Devil eggs by slicing lengthwise and removing yolks. Mash yolks with mayonnaise, spicy mustard, 6 drops Tabasco sauce, lemon juice and pepper. Stuff egg whites with yolk mixture and place in bottom of casserole. Make white sauce recipe of your choice. Add chopped beef and seasonings to taste. Gently pour over eggs. Sprinkle with Parmesan cheese. Bake at 350° for 30 minutes. Makes 8 - 10 servings.

THE HOUSE ON THE HILL is a Victorian farmhouse near a quiet village overlooking the beautiful "Chain of Lakes," in the resort region of northern Michigan, with year-round recreation and great dining. The area is known for seasonal spectaculars - morels and wildflowers in Spring, succulent Summer fruits and vegetables, magnificent Fall colour, and a Winter wonderland. All summer and winter activities including antiquing, winery tours and Mackinac Island are nearby. A picture postcard view may be enjoyed from the splendid veranda. The 5 guest rooms are furnished with period antiques, queen beds, and all modern amenities. Share a delicious Texas breakfast with your hosts. From the inn's hilltop perch, the landscape slopes toward St. Clair Lake and two world class restaurants, Tapawingo and Rowe Inn, both within walking distance. Y'all come!

To receive more information about HOUSE ON THE HILL write or call:
Box 206, Ellsworth, MI 49729 (616) 588-6304

THREE-CHEESE EGG PIES

1 pkg. Jiffy pie dough mix
1 pkg. shredded Cheddar cheese
1 pkg. shredded Monterey Jack cheese
1 pkg. shredded Swiss cheese
7 eggs
3/4 cup cream or half & half
Parsley flakes

Make pie dough mix according to directions on package. Form into individual 2" balls (can get 12 - 14 balls out of one package). Freeze those you don't use. Roll out 6 individual dough balls on floured surface (being careful not to crease or tear) until 6" - 8" in diameter. Carefully form each pie shell into oversize (Texas) muffin pan. Trim and fold over edges as you would for a pie. Mix cheeses together. Fill each pie crust with cheese mix half full. Beat eggs and cream, pour into each pie, filling to 1/4" from top. Bake at 375° for 20 - 25 minutes until crested and just browning on top. Pies will rise and then collapse when out of the oven. Garnish with parsley. Let sit for 5 minutes before serving. Makes 6 servings. NOTE: The recipe usually takes 1 more egg than the number of pies you make. You can use egg substitute and water for the eggs and cream.

THE RICHARDI HOUSE is a Grand 1895 Victorian mansion with period antiques throughout. Listed on the National Register, the house features etched glass window, birds-eye maple woodwork, handpainted ceiling decor and original lighting fixtures. THE RICHARDI HOUSE is located in a beautiful four-season resort region of northwest Michigan, halfway between Traverse City and Petoskey. Minutes to championship golf courses and some of the Midwest's finest downhill and cross-country skiing (Shanty/Schuss and Boyne Mountain Resorts). Just one block to downtown Bellaire for Victorian style antique shops and gift boutiques. Enjoy a stroll along the new brick sidewalks where Victorian streetlamps light the downtown district. We are adjacent to Richardi Park for swimming, tennis, basketball, and a playground.

To receive more information about RICHARDI HOUSE write or call:
402 N. Bridge St., Bellaire, MI 49615 (616) 533-6111

VEGETABLE QUICHE

Crust:
1 stick oleo
1 cup flour
1/2 teaspoon salt

Filling:
4 eggs
1 cup half & half
1/4 teaspoon dry mustard
Dash of pepper
1/4 teaspoon garlic powder
Sweet basil to taste
1 cup frozen Oriental vegetables, pre-cooked or microwaved
1 cup shredded cheese (any variety)
Nutmeg

Blend together crust ingredients, and pat with hands into 9" quiche dish. Bake 7 minutes at 350°. Beat eggs with a whisk. Add half & half, dry mustard, pepper, garlic powder and sweet basil. Place vegetables and cheese in bottom of partially baked crust. Pour egg mixture over crust. Sprinkle with nutmeg. Bake at 350° for 40 minutes. Makes 6 servings.

Our 1860's Greek Revival was built by Crosby Eaton who was a farmer, educator, and State Representative. Over the years the house had been a guest house, an art colony, and after many ownerships, had fallen into a state of disrepair. In 1986 we established A COUNTRY PLACE B&B where it is once again serving up warm hospitality and comfortable accommodations. The peaceful surroundings make a perfect spot to get away from it all. A recent guest was sent here for a rest by her husband. She was a mother of 3 teens, a substitute teacher, and a physician's wife! During her stay she noticed our kitchen table that had 5 coats of paint, even though it was hidden by a quilt. On the day my guest checked out, she took the table with her to refinish. Ten weeks later my beautifully restored kitchen table was returned, sending the quilt back to the closet.

To receive more information about A COUNTRY PLACE B&B write or call: Rt. 5, Box 43, N. Shore Drive, South Haven, MI 49090
(616) 637-5523

ZUCCHINI QUICHE

6 eggs
1/2 cup cream
1 cup shredded Cheddar cheese
8 strips crumbled, cooked bacon
2 cups grated zucchini
1 tablespoon dried onion
1 tablespoon salt
Pepper to taste
1 tablespoon dry mustard
1/2 cup shredded Swiss cheese
Phyllo dough for crust

Mix eggs and cream. Add the remainder of ingredients, except Swiss, and mix. Top with Swiss cheese. Line buttered pie plate with buttered phyllo dough. Add filling. Bake at 375° for 45 minutes. Makes 8 servings.

Origin: This is an original recipe. My guests love it served with homemade bread.

In 1874 our beautiful BOYDEN HOUSE was built and bore the only bathroom in town!!! Boyden children and grandchildren have treasured their memories in Grand Haven and continue to visit the "House" each summer. Our greatest joy is the comfort our guests appreciate while visiting us. One, of our many, special memories is of the guest who gave a passerby a tour of our home while we were at church. She guided her through, and offered her coffee and a muffin. What a pleasant surprise to find out that the passerby was a travel writer, and oh, how we benefited from her articles! We love our BOYDEN HOUSE INN BED & BREAKFAST and our nicest return comes when our guests show us they do, too!

To receive more information about BOYDEN HOUSE B&B write or call: 301 South Fifth, Grand Haven, MI 49417 (616) 846-3538

ASSORTED BAKED GOODS

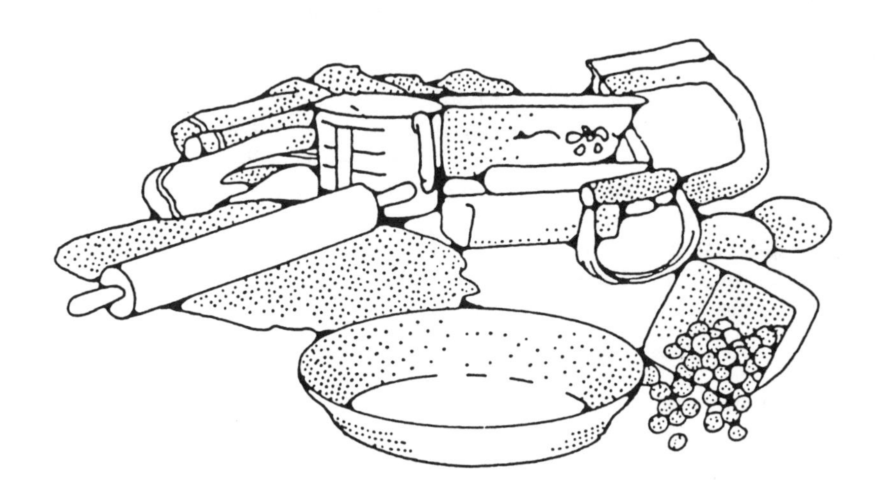

APPLE-ALMOND KUCHEN

Crust:
1 1/2 cups flour
1/3 cup sugar
3/4 teaspoon baking powder
7 tablespoons butter or margarine
1/2 teaspoon vanilla
1 large egg

Filling:
2 tablespoons margarine or butter
1/2 cup almonds
1/2 cup sugar
3 tablespoons flour
1 large egg
1/2 teaspoon vanilla
3 Golden Delicious apples

Heat oven to 350°. Use 9" - 9 1/2" springform pan. To make crust, use food processor: process flour, sugar, and baking powder. Add butter and process until like coarse crumbs. Add egg and vanilla and process until it makes a soft dough. Spread in bottom of pan and up side about 1". Refrigerate. Filling: Place margarine, almonds, sugar, flour, egg, and vanilla in food processor. Process one minute. Spread over crust. Peel, quarter or slice apples, arrange over filling in a petal fashion. Bake 60 - 65 minutes. Cover and cool. May be refrigerated up to 3 days. Makes 10 servings.

One of the most enjoyable things we have in our inn is our "Bathroom Guest Book." Many of our guests jot down their thoughts and opinions. We hear everything from poems to praise about our B&B. It brings us a lot of laughter and enjoyment. We would highly recommend that other innkeepers place one in their baths!

To receive more information about PENTWATER INN write or call:
180 E Lowell, Pentwater, MI 49449 (616) 869-5909

BANANA BREAD

1/2 cup butter or margarine
1 cup sugar
2 eggs
1 teaspoon baking soda
2 cups flour
1/4 teaspoon salt
1/2 cup chopped nuts
3 ripe bananas, sliced

Cream butter, sugar, and eggs. Add dry ingredients. Lift beaters and beat bananas in separate bowl. Add to creamed mixture and mix well. Add nuts. Pour into 2 - 3 1/4" x 7" loaf pans which have been greased. Bake at 375° for 45 - 60 minutes. Makes 2 loaves.

Origin: My mother-in-law, Mary Rummel, who was a super baker, gave me this recipe. Many of my guests look for it on their return visits.

TREE HAVEN, originally The Beck House, was built around 1876. Although in the village of Sebewaing, the large lot and many trees give it an air of privacy. Our front porch embraces one of the four huge maples gracing the front lawn. We have a picture of our home taken about 125 years ago showing the trees as mere saplings. Many of our guests have referred to their stay as "coming home".

To receive more information about RUMMEL'S TREE HAVEN write or call: 41 N. Beck St. (M-25), Sebewaing, MI 48759 (517) 883-2450

BISCUIT MOLD

Chopped nuts
1/2 cup butter, melted
1 tablespoon syrup
1/2 cup brown sugar
Refrigerator biscuits to fill a 5-cup mold

Sprinkle nuts on the bottom of a 5-cup mold. Pour butter, syrup and brown sugar over nuts. Stand biscuits up in the pan. Bake at 375° for 25 - 30 minutes. Invert on serving platter. Makes 4 - 5 servings.

Origin: This has been a staple at HIDDEN POND since the start.

HIDDEN POND is a lovely retreat in the peaceful countryside of west Michigan. Set on 28 acres of woods and fields, perfect for relaxation and tranquility. 2 rooms of quiet elegance to serve your slow-paced overnight. Recently a family came to relive memories of yesterday. The husband/father had just passed on and they had returned to where they all came for get-aways. The trip helped the family ease the pain of their loss. Talking with them and helping them made us understand even more what professional innkeeping means to your guests.

To receive more information about HIDDEN POND B&B write or call:
5975 128th Avenue, Fennville, MI 49408 (616) 561-2491

BLUEBERRY COFFEE CAKE

3/4 cup sugar
1/4 cup shortening
1 egg
1/2 cup milk
2 cups flour
2 teaspoons baking powder
1/2 teaspoon salt
2 cups blueberries

Topping:
1/2 cup sugar
1/3 cup flour
1/2 teaspoon cinnamon
1/4 cup soft butter

Heat oven to 375°. Grease and flour square pan, 9" x 9" x 1 3/4". Mix sugar, shortening, and egg thoroughly. Stir in milk. Measure flour. Blend dry ingredients, stir into wet ingredients. Carefully fold in blueberries. Spread batter in pan. Sprinkle top with mixture of topping ingredients. Bake 45 - 50 minutes. Makes 9 - 3" squares.

THE AMERICAN INN was built in 1896, by Franklin Drury, owner of a large hardware store that serviced the area lumber mills. Shortly after opening our B&B, my husband's brother stayed overnight. Early the next morning, the builder's great-grandson, Frank Drury, came by to tour our inn. When Ed got up and glanced at the guest book, he was startled to see Frank's name, knowing the history of our inn! He was sure we had a resident ghost!

To receive more information about THE AMERICAN INN write or call:
312 E. Cass, Cadillac, MI 49601 (616) 779-9000

BUBBLE BREAD COFFEE CAKE

1 loaf frozen bread
1/2 pkg. (6 oz.) butterscotch chips
1 cup chopped nuts
1 stick melted margarine
1/2 pkg. instant butterscotch pudding
1/2 cup packed brown sugar
1 1/2 teaspoons cinnamon

Thaw bread dough for one hour, then cut into pieces. Place chopped nuts and butterscotch chips in a buttered bundt pan. Then add pieces of bread. Pour melted margarine over dough. Mix dry pudding, brown sugar, and cinnamon and sprinkle on top. Cover with foil. Let rise for one hour, and place in refrigerator overnight. In the morning, bake at 350° for 30 minutes.

Origin: I am also a nurse; 1 of my regular patients brings me a favorite recipe each time she's readmitted, to share with our B&B guests.

SEASCAPE's private beach is located directly on the sandy shore of Lake Michigan, 400' north of the Grand Haven Harbor. Guests always comment on how quiet and relaxing our lakefront rooms are. One beautiful summer evening a couple of guests fell asleep on our deck while watching the sunset. Lulled by the peaceful rhythm of the waves lapping the shore and the gentle lake breeze, they slept until 7:30 in the morning. They awoke to the sound of the fog horn. Having been told of our breakfast bell we ring each morning when breakfast is on the table, they visualized all the other guests sitting around the deck tables watching them sleep. Sheepishly they opened their eyes to find no one up, and went to their room.

To receive more information about SEASCAPE B&B write or call:
20009 Breton, Spring Lake, MI 49456 (616) 842-8409

CARROT-COCONUT BREAD

3 eggs, room temperature
1/2 cup oil
1 teaspoon vanilla
2 cups shredded carrots
2 cups coconut
1 cup raisins
1 cup chopped walnuts
2 cups flour
1 teaspoon baking soda
1 teaspoon baking powder
1 teaspoon cinnamon
1/2 teaspoon salt
1 cup sugar

In large mixing bowl, beat eggs until light in color. Stir in oil and vanilla. Blend in carrots, coconut, raisins and nuts. Stir in flour, baking soda and powder, cinnamon, salt, and sugar. Stir only until mixture is well-blended. Spoon batter into well-greased 9" x 5" loaf pan. Bake at 350° for one hour or until loaf is golden brown and toothpick inserted in center comes out clean. Remove loaf from pan, cool on wire rack. Mature in refrigerator 2 - 3 days before serving. Makes 1 loaf.

With stained glass windows and nine fireplaces, this 1889 historical English Tudor home is indeed an elegant journey into the past. Because its magnificent open foyer and oak staircase lend themselves so beautifully to many small weddings, and family gatherings, one bride felt she was not the center of attraction (even though she really was). Original features include speaking tubes, a warming oven, and gas and electric chantillers. A clawfoot tub is a favorite of a 6' 8" guest who says he comes for his annual bath!

To receive more information about STONEHEDGE INN B&B write or call: 924 Center Ave. (M-25), Bay City, MI 48708 (517) 894-4342

CHERRY BRUNCH

1 stick oleo (1/2 cup)
1 cup sugar
2 eggs
1 teaspoon vanilla
2 cups flour
1/2 teaspoon soda
1/2 teaspoon baking powder
1/2 teaspoon salt
1 cup sour cream
1 can sour cherry pie filling

Topping:
1/3 cup sugar
1/3 cup brown sugar
1/2 cup flour
1 teaspoon cinnamon
1/3 cup chopped nuts
1/3 cup oleo

Cream shortening, sugar, eggs, and vanilla. Measure flour and sift together flour, soda, baking powder and salt. Combine with first mixture along with sour cream. Spread half of batter in bottom of greased and floured 9" x 13" pan. On top of this spread 1 can sour cherry pie filling, then top with remaining batter. Mix topping ingredients together, and top cake with crumb topping. Bake at 350° for 45 minutes to 1 hour. Check with toothpick.

Origin: A favorite recipe taken from the local newspaper, which won an award for best cherry coffee cake at the National Cherry Festival!

One of Traverse City's newest B&B's is MISSION POINT B&B. Situated on West Grand Traverse Bay within walking distance of an historic lighthouse, guests enjoy a Williamsburg estate-like setting as well as the white sand beach and spectacular bay front sunsets. Nestled under down comforters and quilts, guests rest to the sound of lapping waves and ceiling fans. One gentleman on vacation from the city said it was like sleeping in a church by the bay. Private baths, TV, phone, beach chairs, and beach towels are guest amenities. Wake to a full country breakfast and homemade coffee cake served outside by the perennial garden or in the dining room.

To receive more information about MISSION POINT B&B write or call:
20202 Center Road, Traverse City, MI 49684 (616) 223-7526

CHERRY COFFEE CAKE

- **1 cup sugar**
- **6 tablespoons butter**
- **1 cup all-purpose flour**
- **1 teaspoon baking powder**
- **2 eggs**
- **1/2 teaspoon vanilla extract**
- **1 1/2 cups sweet cherries, pitted & halved**
- **1 tablespoon brown sugar**
- **1/4 teaspoon cinnamon**

Preheat oven to 350°. Grease 9" springform pan. In mixer bowl, beat sugar and butter until light and fluffy. Add flour, baking powder, eggs, and vanilla; beat until well combined. Spread in pan. Place cherry halves on batter. Sprinkle with brown sugar and cinnamon mixture. Bake 1 hour. Cool cake in pan. Makes 8 servings.

LEE POINT INN B&B brings the outdoors inside with its gorgeous view of the bay, beautiful woods, cherry orchards, and flower-filled decks. A private sandy beach offers swimming, and relaxation. This beautiful traditional farmhouse-style home renders charm & comfort in a secluded, peaceful country setting. 3 guest rooms overlook the water, with comfortably decorated living areas where guests can relax & socialize. A delicious full breakfast is served on the deck by the bay or in the formal dining room. A house favorite, "Cherry Coffee Cake," made with cherries indigenous to our cherry capital area, is often part of the fare. Located between Traverse City and Suttons Bay, we are convenient to summer and winter activities, local wineries, fine dining, marinas, and shopping. When guests pack up to leave, they also pack up fond memories to take with them - that is the goal of innkeepers Fred & Patty Kilbourn for each and every guest.

To receive more information about LEE POINT INN B&B ON WEST GRAND TRAVERSE BAY write or call: 2885 S. Lee Point Lane, Suttons Bay, MI 49682 (616) 271-6770

CRANBERRY COFFEE CAKE

- **2 cups flour**
- **1 teaspoon baking powder**
- **1 teaspoon baking soda**
- **1/2 teaspoon salt**
- **1/2 cup butter or margarine**
- **1 cup sugar**
- **2 large eggs**
- **1 teaspoon almond extract**
- **1/2 pt. sour cream (8 oz.)**
- **8 oz. whole cranberry sauce**
- **1/2 cup almonds**

Mix dry ingredients. Beat butter and sugar, add eggs, beat well. Add almond extract. Mix mixture with dry ingredients and sour cream. Spoon half of batter into greased bundt pan. Add half of the cranberry sauce. Swirl. Add remaining batter and cranberry sauce on top. Sprinkle with almonds. Makes 12 servings.

THE VILLAGE ROSE B&B, renovated and opened 2 years ago, was built in 1901. Located in Rockford, an old mill town, the home sits on a maple-lined street. Recently, one of our guests reserved a room in order to attend the 50th Rockford High School reunion. As we sat together on our porch, she revealed that she had been the <u>teacher</u> for the class. At 87, she is one of our most delightful and interesting guests.

To receive more information about VILLAGE ROSE B&B write or call:
161 N. Monroe, Rockford, MI 49341 (616) 866-7041

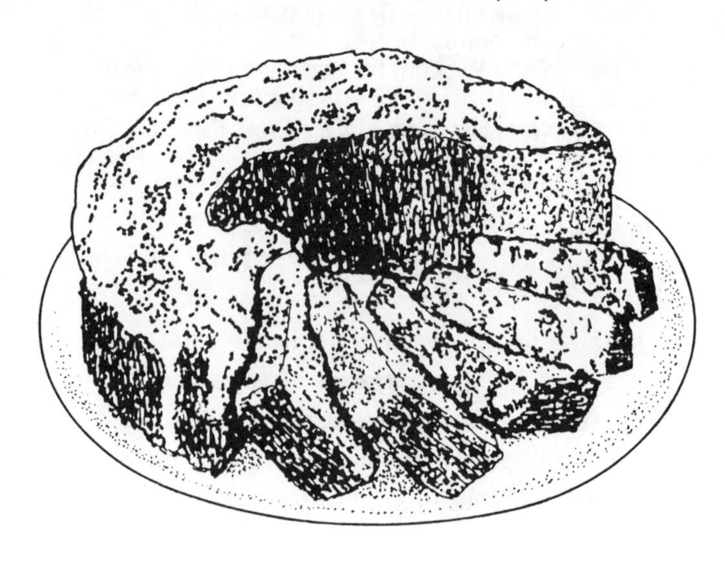

DANISH PASTRY

1 yeast cake
1/2 cup lukewarm water
1 cup shortening
3 tablespoons sugar
1 teaspoon salt
4 cups flour
1 cup scalded milk
2 eggs, separated

Filling:
1 can crushed pineapple
1 cup sugar
1 tablespoon cornstarch

Dissolve yeast in warm water. Mix shortening, sugar, salt, and flour as for pie crust. Beat egg yolks. Add scalded milk and yeast mixture to dough. Add dough mixture and yolks to flour and beat well. Cover and place in cool place overnight. Divide into three parts. Roll out, brush with slightly beaten egg white and fill with fruit filling in the middle. Cut slits in dough 3" long, 1 1/2" apart. Fold dough over fruit. Let rise for 1 hour or until it increases to half again its size. Bake at 350° for 25 - 30 minutes. Makes 36 pieces.

Origin: Passed down through my family for about four generations.

Wildcat Bob rolled into our parking lot in an eighteen-wheeler one night. That night, every time our hand-carved walnut Gazo grandfather's clock chimed, we heard a chorus of wild animal calls. One of our guests, a cat enthusiast, heard "purring" on our slate patio, and went out to pet the cat. Two seconds later, the guest returned, white as a sheet. "You've got a cougar out there!" I said, "I know - I park our car out back every night." "No, you don't understand, this is a real live cougar with claws!" At this point, Wildcat Bob ran outside to coax the reluctant cougar back to the truck with a thick juicy steak, while we watched from the safety of our cherry wood game room. Bob apologized for the commotion Lucy the cougar had caused, and we all slept a little better knowing she was well fed.

To receive more information about GIBSON HOUSE B&B, write or call: 311 W. Washington, Greenville, MI 48838 (616) 754-6691

DANISH PUFF COFFEE CAKE

1 stick oleo
1 cup flour
2 tablespoons water
1 stick oleo
1 cup water
1 cup flour
1 teaspoon almond flavoring
3 eggs
Chopped nuts

Mix 1 stick oleo, 1 cup flour and 2 tablespoons water, and press out into 2 long strips onto an ungreased cookie sheet. Bring 1 stick oleo and 1 cup water to a boil. Remove from heat. Add to water 1 cup flour, almond flavoring and eggs, one at at time, mixing well. Spread this mixture atop dough strips with a spatula. Bake at 350° for approximately 1 hour, or until light brown. Cool. Frost with any cream icing, and top with nuts. Makes 20 pieces.

Origin: My daughter makes this for Victorian tea parties.

Our inn was built in 1895 and was lived in by the same family for many years. We are new to this area, and very interested in hearing the history of our home. The 91 year old granddaughter of the builder of our place lives here in Gaylord, and one day we had her over for tea and conversation. This lovely lady brought over pictures and keepsakes for us to see. She remembers visiting here as a child and her grandmother would give the children each a "goodie": she would cut a pink peppermint candy along the scored line and give each child a half as a treat.

To receive more information about HERITAGE HOUSE B&B write or call: 521 E. Main, Gaylord, MI 49735 (517) 732-1199

LEMON BREAD

2 cups sugar
1 stick butter or margarine
Grated rind of 2 lemons
3 eggs
3 cups flour
2 teaspoons baking powder
1/2 teaspoon salt
1 cup nuts (pecans or walnuts)
1 cup milk

Lemon Glaze:
1/4 cup sugar
1/2 cup lemon juice

Cream sugar, butter, and lemon rind. Add eggs, beat well. Sift dry ingredients together. Add to creamed mixture, alternating with milk. Spread batter into 2 well-greased loaf pans or a 10" tube pan. Bake at 350° for 50 minutes. Remove from pans and place on plate. Pour Lemon Glaze over the top and sides of loaf. Cool thoroughly before cutting. Makes 10 - 12 servings.

THE GINGERBREAD HOUSE has accommodated summer guests since the early days of the century. It has been a cherished summer cottage by its owners and guests alike over the course of its history. One of 435 summer cottages built before 1900 as part of the Bay View Association, THE GINGERBREAD HOUSE is located on Little Traverse Bay in Petoskey.

To receive more information about THE GINGERBREAD HOUSE write or call: P.O. Box 1273, 205 Bluff, Bay View, MI 49770
(616) 347-3538

PEACH COFFEE CAKE

1 pkg. yeast
1/4 cup warm water
2 1/2 cups flour
1 teaspoon salt
2 tablespoons sugar
1/2 cup butter or oleo
1/4 cup evaporated milk
1 unbeaten egg
Peach jam

Soften yeast in warm water, set aside. Mix flour, sugar, and salt in bowl. Cut in butter (oleo) until particles are fine. Add milk, yeast mixture, and egg and mix well. Cover and chill 2 hours or overnight. Divide dough approximately in half. Roll out larger piece to fit 10" x 15" x 1" jelly roll pan. Spread with peach jam (or your choice of jam, jelly or preserves). Roll out second piece of dough quite thin. Cut strips and place in latticework design over jam. Let rise for half an hour. Bake at 350° for 30 minutes.

Origin: From a friend whose aunt had cooked for a wealthy family in St. Louis, MO area many, many years ago.

We have no favorite story about a guest, all our guests have been most delightful. The comment we hear most about the house is "It's just like my grandmother's." An 1880 farmhouse, listed on the Register of National Historic Structures, filled with antiques and an atmosphere of "what used to be". No smoking, pets or credit cards. We have 3 rooms with a bath "down the hall".

To receive more information about THE COURTYARD write or call:
G-3202 W. Court St., Flint, MI 48532 (313) 238-5510

PEACHY CHEESE COFFEE CAKE

- **3/4 cup flour**
- **1 teaspoon baking powder**
- **1/2 teaspoon salt**
- **1 pkg. vanilla pudding mix (not instant)**
- **3 tablespoons butter or margarine, melted**
- **1 egg**
- **1/2 cup milk**
- **Sliced, canned, drained peaches (reserve juice)**
- **8 oz. ricotta cheese**
- **1/2 cup sugar**
- **2 tablespoons peach juice**
- **1 tablespoon sugar**
- **1/2 teaspoon cinnamon**

Beat together first 7 ingredients, for about 2 minutes. Pour into greased 10" pie pan. Arrange peaches over dough. Combine cheese, sugar and peach juice, and spoon over peaches, leaving 1" edges. Combine sugar and cinnamon, and sprinkle on top. Bake at 350° for 25 - 35 minutes. Makes 8 servings. NOTE: We substitute ricotta cheese for cream cheese to reduce fat. Also can use strawberries or pineapple instead of peaches.

THE DUTCH COLONIAL INN was built in 1928. Owners Bob and Pat Elenbaas began the business in 1988. The Bed & Breakfast was their attempt to fill the void in the home after their children moved out. The Elenbaas' welcome guests into their home; in fact, the inn's motto is, "Our home is your home." Some guests truly take this to heart. One business lady, who stays a few nights a week, is so much at home she leaves her cosmetics in "her" room and has even borrowed the innkeeper's clothes on occasion. This guest also encourages other travelers to stay at the DUTCH COLONIAL INN, claiming they will love it as it has become her home away from home.

To receive more information about DUTCH COLONIAL INN write or call: 560 Central Ave., Holland, MI 49423 (616) 396-3664

PLUM GOODIE COFFEE CAKE

1 1/4 cups flour
3/4 cup sugar
2 teaspoons baking powder
1/2 teaspoon salt
6 tablespoons butter
1 beaten egg
1/4 cup milk
1/2 teaspoon rum extract
Plums, to taste
1/3 cup flour
2 tablespoons soft butter
4 tablespoons brown sugar
1/2 teaspoon cinnamon

Frosting:
1 tablespoon melted butter
Powdered sugar
Milk
1/2 teaspoon rum extract

Blend flour, sugar, baking powder, salt, and butter until crumbly. Add egg, milk, and rum extract. Spread mixture in bottom of a greased 9" springform pan. Top with pitted and sliced plums to taste. Combine flour, soft butter, brown sugar, and cinnamon, and sprinkle over plums. Bake at 375° for approximately 40 minutes, depending on how juicy the plums are. Cool slightly. Remove sides from pan and place cake on a serving plate. Make a thin frosting and drizzle over the coffee cake. Slice and serve. Makes 8 - 10 servings.

SOUTH CLIFF INN is located on a bluff overlooking Lake Michigan and is also located on the major highway into St. Joseph. People are occasionally concerned that it may be noisy because of traffic, but after 7 P.M. the traffic is minimal. One guest said that the only reason she came was because her husband made her, and that she never slept well away from home. Of course, I was concerned, but to make a long story short, they missed breakfast at 10 A.M. and didn't arise until almost noon. She said she had not slept that well in years, and wanted to know what kind of sedatives I put in the pillows! She also said she had never slept in a more comfortable bed, as well as environment. Needless to say, they are now regular guests.

To receive more information about SOUTH CLIFF INN write or call:
1900 Lakeshore Drive, St. Joseph, MI 49085 (616) 983-4881

PUMPKIN BREAD

2 cups sugar
1 cup vegetable oil
4 large eggs
1/2 cup water
3 1/2 cups all-purpose flour
4 teaspoons cinnamon
2 teaspoons baking soda
1 teaspoon salt
1/2 teaspoon ground cloves
2 cups canned pumpkin
1 cup chopped pecans
1/2 cup raisins

Preheat oven to 350°. Grease 2 - 9" x 5" loaf pans. Combine sugar and oil in large mixing bowl. Beat in eggs one at a time. Mix in water. Sift together flour and next 4 ingredients. Stir in egg mixture. Mix in pumpkin. Stir in pecans and raisins. Divide batter between prepared pans. Bake until tester comes out clean, about 1 hour. Cool bread in pan 10 minutes. Turn out onto racks and cool completely. Can be prepared ahead. Wrap loaves tightly and refrigerate 2 days or freeze 1 month.

THE CHICAGO PIKE INN is an elegant Colonial Reformed House built in 1903. My favorite guest story is about a couple who came on a cold winter's night in February to stay at the inn. About 6:00 they came down dressed formally for dinner. I thought they were going out on the town for a special evening. About 6:45 they were back. Surprised, I asked them where they went in such a short time! They replied, "Big Boy", because they wanted to be able to spend the evening enjoying all of the rooms in the house. They then sat and enjoyed the lit candles spread about, the glowing fireplaces, and the quiet elegance of the inn.

To receive more information about CHICAGO PIKE INN write or call:
215 East Chicago Street, Coldwater, MI 49036 (517) 279-8744

SOUR CREAM - CINNAMON BREAKFAST CAKE

4 eggs
1/2 cup sugar
3/4 cup vegetable oil
1 box yellow cake mix
1 cup sour cream
3/4 cup walnuts, chopped
1/4 cup dark brown sugar
1 tablespoon cinnamon
Powdered sugar

Beat eggs until thick and fluffy, approximately 3 minutes. Add white sugar, and oil, and beat again. Blend in the cake mix, sour cream, and nuts. Pour half of the batter into a well-greased bundt pan. Mix together brown sugar and cinnamon and sprinkle over the batter. Swirl it in lightly with a knife. Pour remaining batter on top. Bake at 350° for 45 - 60 minutes. Unmold and dust with powdered sugar.

Vera and John McKown, owners of THE BRIDGE STREET INN in Charlevoix, say that their Sour Cream-Cinnamon Cake is a favorite with their guests. We have been in business since 1988. The inn was restored in 1989 with an English motif. Truly a four season inn. Whether you crave a restful getaway or action-packed vacation, we will make your stay a memorable one.

To receive more information about THE BRIDGE STREET INN write or call: 113 Michigan Avenue, Charlevoix, MI 49720 (616) 547-6606

SPICE COFFEE CAKE

2 cups flour
1 cup sugar
1/2 teaspoon cloves
1 teaspoon nutmeg
1 teaspoon cinnamon
1/2 teaspoon salt
1/2 cup shortening
1 egg, beaten
1 tablespoon molasses
1 cup sour milk
1 teaspoon baking soda

Mix together flour, sugar, cloves, nutmeg, cinnamon, salt, and shortening. Take out 1/2 cup for topping. Add to remainder of batter the egg, molasses, sour milk, and baking soda. Bake in 9" x 9" pan, at 350° for 40 - 45 minutes. Makes 6 - 9 pieces.

Origin: My mother, Elinor Glynn, had this recipe for many years.

THE GOVERNOR'S INN was the summer home of Michigan Governor Albert E. Sleeper (1917 - 1921) and his wife, Mary Moore Sleeper. The couple were childless, but took pleasure in "treating" the neighborhood children to lemonade and cookies on the house's wraparound porches. This august couple, who had met presidents and kings, were pleased to be known as Uncle Bert and Miss Mary to the young people of Lexington.

To receive more information about GOVERNOR'S INN B&B write or call: P.O. Box 471, Lexington, MI 48450 (313) 359-5770

THE TALL SHIP MALABAR MOCHA SWIRL COFFEE CAKE

1 lb. sweet butter (soft)
3 cups white sugar
6 eggs
1 cup cold black coffee (double strength)
2 teaspoons rum extract or vanilla extract
4 cups unbleached white flour
1 tablespoon baking powder
1 cup melted chocolate
Chopped nuts (opt.)

Cream together butter and sugar until smooth. Add eggs one at a time, beating well after each addition. Set aside. Sift together flour and baking powder. Mix coffee and extract. Add flour mixture and coffee mixture alternately to egg mixture, beating by hand. Start with flour and end with flour. Remove 1/3 of final product and blend chocolate into that. Add nuts if desired. Divide first mixture into 2 greased and floured bundt pans, then swirl chocolate mixture into them. Bake at 350° for 45 minutes. Glaze while warm, if desired. Makes 2 cakes.

Living and cooking on a schooner is a unique experience in itself. It never ceases to baffle me that the two questions I'm most often asked by passengers, while I'm at work in the galley, are: "Where do you actually live?" and "You don't really have to cook here, do you? It's just for show?" I politely respond, "Our seven person crew actually lives on board, and if they want 3 meals a day, I really have to cook!" This always leaves me tempted to visit these people at their homes around dinner time and ask them the same questions.

To receive more information about THE TALL SHIP MALABAR write or call: 13390 S.W. Bay Shore Drive, Traverse City, MI 49684 (616) 941-2000

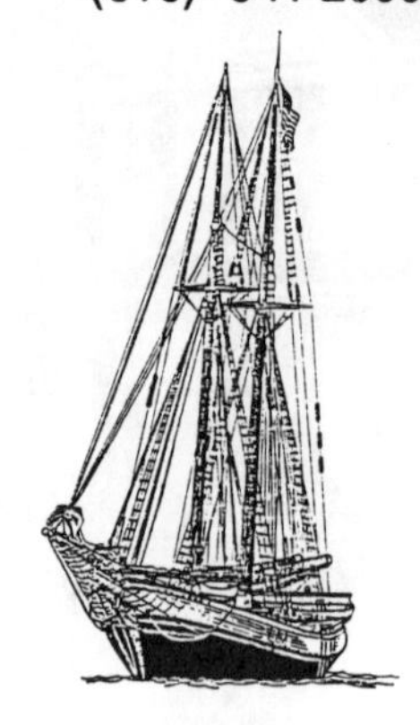

TOASTED ALMOND STICKY BUNS

- 1/2 cup brown sugar
- 2 teaspoons flour
- 2 tablespoons softened margarine
- 1 tablespoon milk
- 1/8 teaspoon almond extract
- 2 - 8 oz. pkgs. crescent dinner rolls
- 1 tablespoon melted margarine
- 1/8 teaspoon almond extract
- 1/4 cup chopped almonds

Glaze:

- 1/2 cup powdered sugar
- 2 - 3 teaspoons milk
- 1/8 teaspoon almond extract

Heat oven to 375°. Combine brown sugar, flour, softened margarine, milk and 1/8 teaspoon almond extract; blend well. Spoon mixture into 12 ungreased muffin cups. Unroll crescent dough into 4 rectangles. Combine melted margarine and 1/8 teaspoon almond extract. Brush onto each rectangle, and sprinkle with almonds. Starting at short side, roll up jelly roll fashion. Cut each roll into 3 slices. Place cut side down in muffin cup. Bake for 15 - 20 minutes. Immediately invert onto wire rack. Combine glaze ingredients. Drizzle over warm sticky buns. Makes 12 rolls.

The Newnham home was built around the turn of the century, purchased by Harry Newnham, one of the "town fathers" in the early 1920's, and occupied by his descendants until the spring of 1985. The exterior of the home is graced with a wraparound porch, complete with "gingerbread" carvings in its corners and a porch swing. Many of our guests spend time reminiscing about their childhood while swinging on the porch swing. We love the charm, history and comfort of this house, and we think you will, too.

To receive more information about THE NEWNHAM SUNCATCHER INN, write or call: 131 Griffith, Saugatuck, MI 49453 (616) 857-4249

CEREALS, FRUITS & BEVERAGES

BERRY-MELON SALAD DRESSING

1/2 cup unsweetened orange juice
1/3 cup unsweetened grapefruit juice
1 tablespoon lemon juice
2 teaspoons vegetable oil
2 tablespoons honey
1 tablespoon cornstarch
1 teaspoon poppy seeds

Combine all ingredients except poppy seeds in a saucepan over medium heat. Stir well. Continue constantly stirring until thickened and bubbly. Stir in poppy seeds. Put into container with cover and chill at least 2 hours, or overnight. Spoon over cut-up fruit, and garnish with mint sprigs if desired. Makes 8 servings. 111 calories per serving.

Our DOLL HOUSE is a small 1900 Victorian home decorated with family heirlooms and cherished antique dolls. We have seven a/c rooms including a bridal suite with whirlpool tub for two. Each room is a different theme and color. Guests are served a full home-cooked "Heart Smart" breakfast, after which they may walk to town, ride our bicycles to the beach, or just relax on the enclosed front porch filled with white wicker furniture. We have six fun-filled "Special Event Weekend" packages during the fall, Christmas, and early winter. Open year round, enjoy our home in today's comfort, surrounded by yesterday's charm. Room rates are $45.00 to $95.00 and we welcome the business traveler.

To receive more information about DOLL HOUSE INN, write or call:
709 E. Ludington Ave., Ludington, MI 49431 (616) 843-2286

BLACK ROCK BAKED OATMEAL

1/3 cup oil
1/2 cup brown sugar
1 large egg, beaten
2 cups quick oats
1/2 teaspoon salt
1 1/2 teaspoons baking powder
3/4 cup milk
Cinnamon to taste (opt.)
1/3 cup raisins (opt.)

Mix oil, brown sugar and beaten egg. Add oats, baking powder, salt, milk, cinnamon, and raisins, and mix well. Pour into greased 9" x 5" or 8" x 8" pan. Bake at 350° for 25 - 30 minutes. Good served with honey, maple syrup, milk, or vanilla ice cream.

THE McCANN HOUSE, built in 1899, is a fine example of Victorian architecture with its open oak staircase and ornate metal ceilings. Built for the young family of Captain John McCann, it was a part of the large Irish settlement at Beaver Island after the departure of the followers of James Jesse Strang in 1857. Host John Runberg is the grandson of the original owner. Joyce and John really enjoyed a guest couple some time ago. They were returning after nearly 50 years of living and studying in Paris, France. Henry is the recipient of a John and Catherine McArthur Foundation Grant. They have written or edited eight books on Medieval Art!

To receive more information about THE McCANN HOUSE write or call: P.O. Box 241, St. James, MI 49782 (616) 448-2387

BREAKFAST BERRY SHORTCAKE

- 1 cup uncooked oats (quick or old-fashioned)
- 1 cup all-purpose flour
- 2 tablespoons sugar
- 1 tablespoon baking powder
- 1 teaspoon grated lemon peel
- 1/2 teaspoon baking soda
- 1/4 cup margarine (1/2 stick)
- 2/3 cup plain lowfat yogurt, or buttermilk
- Strawberries or blueberries

Combine oats, flour, sugar, baking powder, lemon peel, and baking soda. Mix well. Cut in margarine until crumbly. Add yogurt, mix just until moistened. Knead on floured surface 10 times. Form into 8" circle or I use a 2" doughnut cutter. Lightly spray cookie sheet with no stick cooking spray or oil lightly. Bake at 400° for 15 - 20 minutes or until golden brown. Serve 1 1/2 circles per person with strawberries/blueberries, etc., with more yogurt and a mint leaf on top. Makes 8 - 10 servings.

Built in 1874, we restored this Victorian diplomat's home: 5' pocket doors, 18" wide pine plank floors, and pine woodwork. We have the original memoirs of the diplomat and his wife, written by their second oldest daughter. We also have the deed of this property from the diplomat. Pictures and documents abound. We are a national and state historic site. Each of 4 bedrooms is named after one of the diplomat's children. We have hosted a mother and daughter who met for the first time in 28 years. The mother was from New York, the daughter who made the reservations, from St. Joseph, Missouri.

To receive more information about BEECHWOOD MANOR B&B write or call: 736 Pleasant St., Box 876, Saugatuck, MI 49453
(616) 857-1587

BREAKFAST CUSTARD

3 eggs, beaten
Scant 1/2 cup sugar (to taste)
3 cups milk
Ground nutmeg

Mix eggs, sugar, and milk well with an electric mixer. Top with ground nutmeg. Put into individual custard dishes to bake at 300° for 1 1/2 hours or until knife comes out clean. Place dishes in a pan of water to bake, for smooth consistency.

Origin: From Mama Esther, my Swedish grandmother, who not only taught me to cook, but also gave me her talent for gardening.

THE PARSONAGE was built in 1908, and has been occupied by 7 different ministers and their families. The present owner, Bonnie McVoy-Verwys and her daughter, Wendy Winslow, opened Holland's first B&B in 1984. Rev. Van Laar's family returned for a family reunion bringing a treasured 1937 photograph of their family. Rev. Hoogstras's son Calvin still checks on the beautiful mimosa tree his father planted 50 years ago in the back yard. Guests enjoy our peaceful, relaxing residential setting near Hope College. AAA approved, featured in Country Folk Art Magazine & Detroit Free Press Travel Tales 1992. A delicious breakfast is served in the formal dining room. One guest sent a lovely book with one of her published poems, enscribed: "To Bonnie - Remembering the good time I had at THE PARSONAGE. You are a gracious hostess. Best wishes, Lucille" We look forward to your visit! Reservations required.

To receive more information about THE PARSONAGE 1908 write or call: 6 East 24th Street, Holland, MI 49423 (616) 396-1316

CARAMEL PEACHES HEATHER HOUSE

4 large peaches, skinned & halved
1 stick butter
6 tablespoons brown sugar
2-4 tablespoons water
1/2 teaspoon powdered ginger
1 cup small strawberries, washed & hulled
1/2 cup washed blueberries

Melt butter, brown sugar and ginger over moderately high heat. Add peaches, cut side down, and cook 5 minutes with butter bubbling. Turn peaches and add 2-4 tablespoons water. Cook 5 more minutes. Spoon peach halves, cut side up, into small footed dishes. Wash berries and hull strawberries. Toss berries in caramel sauce for 2 - 3 minutes over moderate heat and spoon over peaches. Divide sauce among servings. Serve warm. Makes 8 servings.

THE HEATHER HOUSE is a lovely 104 year old Queen Anne Victorian home sitting back from the Blue St. Clair River which marks the boundary of the U.S.A. and Canada. The home has 3 lovely guest rooms with private baths. A wonderful get away to restore romance and tranquility to your busy life. One young newlywed couple spent 4 hours over breakfast in our tower nook and had to be persuaded to leave in time to catch a flight to Hawaii!

To receive more information about HEATHER HOUSE write or call:
409 N. Main St., Marine City, MI 48039 (313) 765-3175

CORNMEAL MUSH

3 1/2 cups boiling water
1 teaspoon salt
1 cup corn meal
1 cup cold water
Bacon grease, butter or corn oil for frying

Bring water to a boil in large heavy saucepan, add salt, and cornmeal mixed with cold water. Return to a boil stirring constantly. Cover and cook over very low heat for half an hour, stirring occasionally. If you want fried mush, pour into buttered loaf pan to set overnight or in refrigerator for several hours. Then slice and dip lightly in flour and fry in just a little bacon grease, butter or corn oil. Serve with maple syrup. Serves 8.

Origin: Grace Robinson Waddell (mother of owners, twin sisters Mary Sutherland and Tish Waddell)

At breakfast one morning a very elderly guest whispered to her daughter, "Give these girls a tip." I said, "Oh, no, that is not necessary." The mother frowned at me and whispered louder, "I said, give these girls a tip!" The daughter looked apologetically at me, and said, "If Mother says, 'Give these girls a tip,' I must give you a tip." She laid two $1.00 bills on the table, and the mother nodded, triumphantly. The mother, who was in her late eighties, had been enthralled with our 3 mannekins dressed in our mother's (who was born in 1887) clothes. Mother was a "saver". We have the shoes she wore on her honeymoon, a political button that says, "I am for Wilson and an eight-hour day," and dozens of old family pictures.

To receive more information about OPEN WINDOWS B&B write or call: P.O. Box 698, Suttons Bay, MI 49682 (616) 271-4300

COUNTRY OATMEAL

Ingredients for cooked oatmeal per package directions (DO NOT use instant)
Peeled apple slices
1 tablespoon sugar
1 teaspoon cinnamon
2 - 3 tablespoons butter
1/4 cup brown sugar
Raisins (opt.)

Prepare cooked oatmeal according to package directions. (NOT instant oatmeal) However, add peeled apple slices, sugar and cinnamon to the boiling water for oatmeal. Pour into a buttered dish. Cool. Cover with plastic wrap and refrigerate overnight. In the morning melt butter and brown sugar in a frying pan. Cut oatmeal into wedges or squares, add to pan and brown slowly on medium heat about 5 minutes. Turn and brown opposite side. Carefully place in warmed serving dish. Top with raisins, and offer half & half with it. Mighty good eatin'!

Origin: For porridge lovers - this recipe is from an old friend named Alma - who passed it on to me, her "berry pickin' friend."

THE FARMSTEAD beckons you to come to us, so we may give you rest. Create a diversion from your daily lifestyle to quiet elegance, either by partaking of our afternoon teatime (celebrated by reservation only), enjoying our scenic grounds, practicing your stroke on our golf green, reliving childhood during our Christmas fantasy light display both indoors and out, or quiet solitude in several common areas. Breakfast is fulfilling, afternoon and evening refreshment includes a constantly full tea and coffeepot brewing especially for you. Our goal: to see you leave us better than whence you came. Anticipated in 1993: Official backyard croquet court.

To receive more information about FARMSTEAD B&B LTD. write or call: 13501 Highland Rd., Hartland, MI 48353 (313) 887-6086

DEB'S GRANOLA

9 cups rolled oats
3 cups coconut
3 cups sliced almonds
3/4 cup honey
3/4 cup melted butter
1 1/2 teaspoons cinnamon
1 teaspoon salt
2 cups raisins

Mix together all ingredients except raisins. Bake on cookie sheet at 350° for 25 - 30 minutes, stirring occasionally. Remove from oven. Stir in raisins. Cool and store in airtight containers.

Nestled in the contours of Michigan's most varied lakeside community, THE INN AT UNION PIER is far removed from the demands of your daily schedule. The Inn's genteel charms create the perfect stage for that often postponed weekend. Or, better yet, it's ideal for an indulgent mid-week holiday. Regardless of the time of year, the Inn is your window to Michigan's glorious four seasons. Whether you've selected The Greathouse, The Cottage of Four Seasons, or The Pierhouse, be assured that each is as unique as the guests we welcome. You'll awaken in the morning relaxed, refreshed and ready for one of the hearty, homemade breakfasts that have become a hallmark of THE INN AT UNION PIER. We hope your stay is one that you will remember fondly for years to come. Welcome!

To receive more information about THE INN AT UNION PIER write or call: P.O. Box 222, 9708 Berrien, Union Pier, MI 49129
(616) 469-4700

FRIED APPLES

3/4 stick cold butter
6 - 8 large cooking apples
1/4 cup white sugar
1/2 cup brown sugar
Cinnamon to taste
Top with pecans for ice cream topping

Put butter in a cold frying pan. Cut unpeeled apples into pie slices, as many as you think you want. Jonathans and Ida Reds are the favorites because they hold their shape better. Sprinkle sugars and cinnamon over the top. Cover pan so apples will steam, and turn the heat on low. Stir occasionally. Let sugars form a caramel topping. Makes 6 - 8 servings. Serve with nuts.

Origin: Patti originated this recipe some 26 years ago for a vanilla ice cream topping with pecans.

Vladimar Kovalenko, a Russian bicyclist, passed through THE LUDINGTON HOUSE in July of 1990. He's traveled over 13,000 miles across the United States and through various other countries, last year alone. Through the U.S., the second time around, he purposely went out of his way to visit us again at THE LUDINGTON HOUSE. At the time of his visit last July, 1991, Vladimar had traveled 8,400 miles in seven months; his goal was to pedal 25,000 miles and go through all 50 states. We're pretty sure that we'll see Vladimar again!

To receive more information about THE LUDINGTON HOUSE B&B
write or call: 501 E. Ludington Ave., Ludington, MI 49431
(800) 827-7869

HOT BUTTERED APPLES

Red or Golden Delicious or Granny Smith apples, cored and sliced
Cinnamon to taste

For each apple add:
1 1/2 tablespoons honey
1 1/2 pats of butter
1 1/2 tablespoons black or golden raisins (opt.)

Combine cored sliced apples with honey, butter and raisins (if desired). Dust heavily with cinnamon and bake, covered, for 1 1/2 minutes at full power in microwave. Test to make sure apples are baked, but still firm, or to your personal preference. Each apple will serve 2 persons as a side-dish at breakfast, lunch or dinner. It's great as a condiment for granola cereal or by itself. May substitute strawberries or raspberries, etc., instead of cinnamon and raisins.

Origin: This recipe, originally from my grandmother, is our most requested, and is an absolute requirement of each breakfast buffet.

THE KIRBY HOUSE has been fortunate to serve many visitors foreign to the U.S. One man from the Netherlands spoke very little English. His wife, however, was quite accomplished. We spent many fun-filled moments chatting at breakfast. After the couple had checked out, he reappeared by my sink with his hand stuck out to shake hands - a somewhat sheepish grin on his face. I dried my hands and clasped his. "Best breakfast EVER in America," he said, in a very stilted manner. It was immediately obvious that he had been in his car rehearsing this speech with his wife as coach. We both burst into laughter. Although our breakfast buffet receives many compliments, I can't think of one that was more sincerely expressed or remembered more fondly.

To receive more information about THE KIRBY HOUSE write or call:
294 W. Center, Box 1174, Saugatuck/Douglas, MI 49453
(616) 857-2904

HOT FRUITED CEREAL

14 cups water
4 cups oats
1 cup oat bran
1/2 cup ground rye berries
1/2 cup ground wheat
1/2 cup sliced almonds
1/2 cup raisins
1/2 cup chopped dates
1/2 cup chopped dried apricots

Bring water to a boil in large kettle. Add grains and cook for 10 minutes, stirring often. Add dried fruit and cook for another 5 minutes. Salt as desired. Serve with your favorite breakfast condiments. Makes 14 servings.

Origin: This wholesome recipe is a favorite of our guests who join us for our "wellness weekends".

VILLAGE PARK B&B is an historic home overlooking the welcoming waters of Spring Lake and Village Park. Picnic area, tennis court, and boat launch for access to Lake Michigan. We have six guest rooms with private baths. Serving the Grand Haven, Spring Lake, and Muskegon areas.

To receive more information about VILLAGE PARK B&B write or call:
60 W. Park Street, Fruitport, MI 49415 (616) 865-6289

PEACHDERRY

24 freestone peaches
1 cup water
2 cinnamon sticks
12 whole cloves
6 whole black peppercorns
4 cups sugar (or more)

Peel and pit peaches, dropping them into vinegar-water to keep them from turning brown. Chop peaches and put into very heavy deep kettle with about 1 cup of water (just enough water to keep from scorching) and the whole spices. Cook slowly for about 45 minutes. Remove cinnamon sticks. Cool slightly and put mixture through a food mill. You should have about 12 cups of juice and fruit puree. Return puree to kettle with sugar. You may add up to 1 cup more of sugar if you like. Cook, for at least one hour, stirring frequently, until mixture is quite thick. Meanwhile, wash and sterilize jars and lids. Pour hot peachderry into hot jars. Wipe rims of jars with clean damp cloth, screw on lids, and immediately invert jars. Turn right side up after about 30 minutes and test for seal. Makes 6 half pints.

Origin: "Peachderry" was an imaginary food we served at dolly's tea parties, and it absolutely never contained peaches!

THE INN AT LUDINGTON is over 100 years old. The best compliment we get from our guests is that they feel at home. We serve locally grown and "Made in Michigan" products whenever possible. Recently a couple from Brazil stayed here to attend the graduation of their son, who was an exchange student at Ludington High School. When they were served an American breakfast of pancakes, they wondered from what the maple syrup was made. When we told them it came from trees, they looked puzzled. We truly felt like cultural ambassadors while describing how maple sap is turned into delicious syrup. We could just imagine them going back home and telling their friends that in the U.S., people put tree sap on their breakfast!

To receive more information about THE INN AT LUDINGTON write or call: 701 E. Ludington Avenue, Ludington, MI 49431
(616) 845-7055

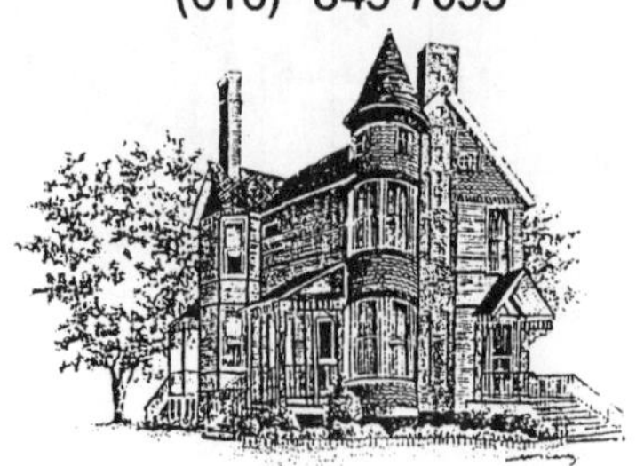

PEACH FRUIT CUPS

1/2 cup vanilla yogurt
1 teaspoon honey
1/8 teaspoon cinnamon
3 large ripe peaches or nectarines, halved & pitted
1 cup fresh blueberries
1 cup fresh raspberries

In small bowl, combine yogurt, honey, and cinnamon; blend well. Spoon 1 tablespoon yogurt mixture onto each serving plate. Top each with 1 peach half, cut side up. Spoon raspberries and blueberries over peach halves. Drizzle with remaining yogurt mixture. Makes 6 servings.

Origin: I don't know the origin of this recipe, but my mom used to serve it to us when we were kids.

THE ROSS HOUSE is the only B&B on the south side of the Black River, just steps from the City's fantastic new marina-park, downtown shopping and the beautiful South Beach. But the location is only one of the nice things about the ROSS HOUSE. Here you can treat yourself to the old country charm that has served as the home to the prominent Ross family for over 90 years. All rooms are uniquely furnished. The lounge provides a comfortable haven after a busy day at the beach. Many fine restaurants are within walking distance. There is a biking-hiking trail nearby.

To receive more information about THE ROSS HOUSE write or call:
229 Michigan Avenue, South Haven, MI 49090 (616) 637-2256

SWEDISH FRUIT

1 lb. pitted prunes (opt.)
1 cup seedless raisins
1 cup currants
1 cup tapioca (large pearl)
3 peeled, sliced apples
1 cup sugar
1 can apricot halves
1 can sliced peaches
1 can sour cherries (or cherry pie filling)
Cinnamon

Soak in water 1" higher than fruit, overnight: prunes, raisins, currants, and tapioca. In the morning, add fresh apple pieces, and cook slowly until tapioca is clear. Then add sugar, apricots, peaches, cherries, and cinnamon, including the fruit juice. 3 sticks of cinnamon can be added and removed after cooking is completed. Serve warmed a little. Very colorful. Makes 3 quarts.

Origin: My father was Swedish, so it is a recipe that has been a family tradition.

THE TIMEKEEPER'S INN was built around 1884 on one of Whitehall's most attractive and old residential streets. The original owner was a "lumber baron" having a lumber mill on the shores of White Lake. Michigan pine, so plentiful in the area, was used in abundance in the construction and decorative interior woodwork of the home. Even the antique tub in the "Black Forest" guest room has a wood rim. Guests often request the "Black Forest" so they can enjoy the great tub! One particular couple who always ride their tandem bike 68 miles to our destination, make a bet with each other on the way. The winner of the bet gets first dibs on a deep bubble bath in that tub!

To receive more information about TIMEKEEPER'S INN, write or call:
303 Mears Ave., Whitehall, MI 49461 (616) 894-5169

NOT JUST FOR BREAKFAST...

BROCCOLI BAKE

- Pastry to make crust for 9" x 13" baking dish
- 4 cups chopped cooked broccoli, cooled
- 2 1/2 cups shredded Cheddar cheese
- 1/4 cup flour
- 6 eggs, slightly beaten
- 1 1/2 cups light cream
- 1/2 teaspoon onion salt
- Dash of white pepper

Roll out pastry to fit 9" x 13" baking pan or a similar size. Sprinkle cooked, cooled broccoli on pastry. Mix cheese and flour, toss gently with broccoli. Combine milk and seasonings, pour over pan. Bake at 350° about 50 minutes or until done. Makes 20 servings.

This was at first a cottage owned by Sylvia A. Stone of Alma, and willed to her heirs in 1925. The cottage was built about 1906 by the Chambers family. The Gage family purchased this home and used it as a resort and tourist home for travelers. We purchased the home in 1989 and completely renovated it with a B&B in mind. Each guest bedroom is individually decorated.

To receive more information about STEVENS' WHITEHOUSE ON THE LAKE write or call 5670 W. Houghton Lake Dr., Houghton Lake, MI 48629 (517) 366-4567

CARAWAY-RYE BREAD

3 tablespoons sugar
2 tablespoons brown sugar
1 tablespoon salt
2 1/2 cups lukewarm water
2 tablespoons molasses
2 cakes compressed yeast (or 2 pkgs.)
2 tablespoons soft shortening
2 tablespoons caraway seeds
2 cups rye flour
6 - 6 1/4 cups all-purpose flour

Mix sugars and salt together. Add liquid and molasses. Add yeast, stir until dissolved. Add shortening, caraway seeds and rye flour. Stir to blend. Add flour in two additions, using the amount necessary to make dough easy to handle. Knead on floured board until dough is smooth and elastic. Place in greased bowl, turning once to grease top. Cover and let rise in warm place, until double. Punch down and let rise again. Punch down and divide dough into two loaves. Place in loaf pans. Let rise again and bake at 375° for 30 - 40 minutes, depending on how brown you like your bread. This bread is delicious toasted or used for a ham sandwich. Leftover coffee can be used for the liquid, making a darker loaf. Makes 2 loaves.

Welcome to Frankenmuth - - enjoy "old-fashioned values" in our ranch-style home, with a spacious yard, surrounded by evergreens, in a quiet residential neighborhood. Homemade breads and jams served family-style, at breakfast. Bedrooms furnished with heirloom quilts, fresh flowers and ceiling fans. Hosts Richard and Donna Hodge enjoy visiting with guests on a wide range of topics including farming, travel, genealogy, fishing, and cooking. Many ideas are exchanged along with tourist flyers and "ancestral charts"! Donna shares her recipes with guests. "Come as a Stranger, leave as a Friend" is the motto at BED & BREAKFAST AT THE PINES.

To receive more information about BED & BREAKFAST AT THE PINES write or call: 327 Ardussi St., Frankenmuth, MI 48734
(517) 652-9019

CHEESE BALL

2 - 8 oz. pkgs. cream cheese
8 oz. sharp Cheddar cheese, shredded
1 tablespoon chopped pimiento
1 tablespoon green pepper, chopped
1 teaspoon chopped onion
2 - 3 teaspoons Worcestershire sauce
2 - 3 tablespoons lemon juice
Dash of salt & pepper
Chopped pecans

Place cream cheese in bowl, and cream it until soft and smooth. Add shredded cheese and mix. Add remainder of ingredients and mix. Shape into a ball. Wrap and chill. Roll in pecans. Makes 6 servings.

We had a guest from London who came to experience American football on every level. As he did not drive, my husband offered to take him to the local high school game. That afternoon I met the teacher who announces the plays in our post office. When I told him about our guest, he took his name and at half-time, introduced him with a flourish, having him stand so the crowd could welcome him. I think there are many advantages in staying with local people!

To receive more information about PAINT CREEK B&B, write or call:
971 Dutton Rd., Rochester Hills, MI 48306 (313) 651-6785

"EMBERS" 1 LB. PORK CHOPS WITH RED SAUCE

6 center-cut pork chops
Marinade:
2 cups soy sauce
1 cup brown sugar
1 tablespoon dark molasses
1 teaspoon salt

Red sauce:
1 tablespoon dry mustard
1/4 cup water
1 cup brown sugar
1 reg. size bottle catsup
1 bottle chili sauce

Mix marinade ingredients and bring to a boil. Marinate each 3" thick pork chop overnight in cooled marinade. Place pork chops in pan, cover tightly with foil. Bake 2 hours at 375°. Combine dry mustard, water, and brown sugar, take out lumps. Then add catsup and chili sauce. When chops are tender, remove from oven. Dip in red sauce and bake at 350° for 30 minutes, uncovered. Lastly, grill for 15 minutes over small bed of coals raised as high as possible. This step can be deleted.

Origin: From Embers Restaurant in Mt. Pleasant, MI, and my mom, Marilyn Barry. It's wonderful!

We have a brand new gazebo/hot tub spa and our guests really enjoy relaxing in it to unwind. Our tame deer are fun for our guests to hand-feed (along with mini horses, sheep, ducks. . .). We have anniversary, wedding night, birthday, and romantic getaway packages that include: a bottle of chilled champagne, fresh-cut flowers, a balloon bouquet, bubble bath, and a lovely continental breakfast. Our central air is nice in summer. And our Vermont Casting stove is cozy to sit by in winter.

To receive more information about COUNTRY CHARM FARM write or call: 5048 Conkey Rd., Caseville, MI 48725 (517) 856-31101

HAM BISCUITS WITH CLOVE HONEY BUTTER

Milk to brush on tops
1 cup flour
2 teaspoons baking powder
1/4 teaspoon salt
1/4 lb. sliced ham, diced
1/2 cup plus 1 tablespoon heavy cream
1/4 cup unsalted butter
1 teaspoon honey
1/8 teaspoon ground cloves

Sift together flour, baking powder, and salt into large bowl. Add ham and cream and stir just until it forms a soft dough. With floured hands, gather dough into a ball, knead it gently 6 times on floured board, and pat out 1/2" thick. Cut out dough into 3" rounds. Place on ungreased baking sheet. Brush biscuit tops with milk. Bake in the middle of the oven at 425° for 15 minutes or until pale gold. Combine unsalted butter, honey, and cloves. Serve with the hot biscuits. Makes 5 biscuits.

Located on the edge of a 124 acre meadowland park, THE URBAN RETREAT B&B combines the conveniences of city living with the delights of a rural setting. As members of the National Wildlife Federation's Backyard Wildlife Habitat program, hosts André Rosalik and Gloria Krys set a bountiful table for all guests, with more than 50 species of birds recorded from their backyard. One summer, after watching the avian activity at the feeders during breakfast, one elderly couple remarked rather wistfully that, in all their years, they had never seen a bluebird. After a short hike into the park, not only were they introduced to their first pair of bluebirds, they also had the pleasure of viewing 5 newly hatched nestlings up close.

To receive more information about THE URBAN RETREAT, write or call: 2759 Canterbury Road, Ann Arbor, MI 48104 (313) 971-8110

ITALIAN CRAB MEAT DIP

8 oz. pkg. & 3 oz. pkg. cream cheese
2 tablespoons mayonnaise
Dash of garlic powder
Dash of Worcestershire sauce
Dash of lemon juice
12 oz. jar chili sauce
Diced onion to taste
6 oz. crab meat, drained
Green parsley for garnish

Blend in blender the cream cheese, mayonnaise, garlic powder, Worcestershire sauce, and lemon juice. Spread onto a 13" - 14" pizza pan. Spread chili sauce on top of cream cheese mixture. Top with diced onion, crab meat, and parsley. Serve with assorted crackers.

Origin: A co-worker brought this dip to a Christmas party in 1979. It's very festive for the holiday season, and it is quick to assemble.

Our 13-room Georgian Colonial home was constructed in 1981 to resemble the original Poulson house, destroyed by fire in 1980. Since our purchase in 1984, many people have visited with us to share their stories of the old Poulson estate. No visit was more captivating, however, than that of Bud Poulson and his wife, Tiffany, from Hinsdale, Illinois. As a young boy, Bud traveled from Chicago to spend summers here with his grandparents. He showed us old family movies of the house, barn, stable, tenant's house, and concrete swimming pool. He also recalled a boxing ring out back which was popular with neighborhood boys during the Joe Lewis era. It sounded like an ideal summer home. The Poulson family split up and sold the estate about 1955.

To receive more information about KAL-HAVEN B&B write or call:
23491 Paulson Rd., Gobles, MI 49055 (616) 628-4932

PEPPER CHEESE SQUARES

1 large pkg. shredded Monterey Jack cheese
1 large pkg. shredded Cheddar cheese
Hot peppers to taste, chopped
Condensed milk

Mix cheeses together. Put half of the cheese in a baking dish, sprinkle hot peppers over the cheese. Add remainder of cheese. Add just enough condensed milk so that you can see it through the cheese. Bake at 375° for 30 minutes. Cool. Cut into squares.

Turn of the century farmhouse on 10 acres with king size beds, down comforters, and lace spreads. Continental breakfast served in a basket at your door. Hot air balloon ride packages available. One of our favorite guest stories is of the son of a former owner of the house calling on Christmas Eve Day. He wanted the loft room that evening to propose to his fiance in the room he had had as a child. She said "yes." "Romance has returned".

To receive more information about THE COUNTRY INN OF GRAND BLANC write or call: 6136 S. Belsay, Grand Blanc, MI 48439
(313) 694-6749

PILLOW POTATO BISCUITS

1/2 cup instant mashed potato flakes
1 teaspoon sugar
2 tablespoons softened butter or margarine
1/2 cup hot water
1/3 cup cold water
3 cups prepared biscuit mix
Milk for tops (opt.)

Combine potato flakes, sugar, butter, and hot water, mix well. Add cold water and biscuit mix, stirring until well-blended. Add a little more cold water if necessary to make a soft dough. Turn out on lightly floured surface; knead about 10 times. Roll dough to 1/2" - 3/4" thick; cut with 2" biscuit cutter or jar lid. Place on ungreased baking sheet. Brush tops with milk. Bake at 450° for about 13 minutes or until lightly browned. Makes 12 biscuits.

Origin: An Orange Park, Florida lady shared this combination she discovered by simply wanting to use up potato flakes left in the box. The result was light and airy biscuits!

Guests have a hard time believing that this modern looking lakefront home is actually over 100 years old. It was one of the first cottages along the lake for those "city" dwellers of Cadillac, a whole four miles away! Of course, roads were scarce then and the only way to get to the cottage was by water. The location has such a spectacular view that the subsequent owners simply expanded and brought it up to date. Today it is a comfortable year round Bed & Breakfast, with guest rooms overlooking Lake Mitchell. Being at the junction of Michigan Roads 115 and 55 makes it centrally located and easy to find! It is truly a four season resort.

To receive more information about ESSENMACHER'S B&B write or call: 204 Locust Lane, Cadillac, MI 49601 (616) 775-3828

POPOVERS

1 1/4 cups milk
1 1/4 cups flour
1/2 teaspoon salt
3 eggs

Pour milk into medium-sized bowl. Add flour and salt. Beat until well-blended. Add eggs, one at a time, beating well after each addition. Pour into greased popover pans and bake in preheated oven at 425° for 20 minutes. Decrease heat to 325° and bake 15 minutes more. Makes 8 popovers.

Origin: This is my mother's recipe, traditionally served with roast beef. We serve it with honey butter with afternoon tea.

Many of our guests came to South Haven as children, and enjoy telling us how it was in the "good old days." They always mention "Apple Molly" who used to sell homemade caramel apples on the beach. We have since discovered that one of our guests has carried on "Apple Molly's" tradition - she is the proud owner of "Mrs. Prindible's" - and her gourmet caramel apples can be found in all the finer department stores.

To receive more information about ARUNDEL HOUSE write or call:
56 North Shore Drive, South Haven, MI 49090 (616) 637-4790

RASPBERRY ALMOND BARS

1 cup butter
1 cup sugar
1 egg
1 teaspoon almond extract
2 1/2 cups flour
1/2 teaspoon baking powder
1/4 teaspoon salt
Raspberry jam

Cream butter and sugar, add egg, and almond extract. Add flour, baking powder and salt. Spread into a 9" square baking dish. Smooth surface using a wet fork. Make 5 diagonal grooves with the back of the fork, and fill them with jam. Bake 15 minutes at 350°. Cool before cutting into small squares. A great almond shortbread! Ideal for tea or late-night snacks.

LINDEN LEA ON LONG LAKE was originally built as a summer lake cottage around the turn of the century. While remodeling and enlarging our home, we removed and rebuilt several walls. One wall contained a can of bedbug lotion and an empty bottle from the Traverse City Brewery. We considered using the name, "Bedbugs and Beer B&B", but <u>not</u> for very long! LINDEN LEA now takes its name from the Lake District in northern England, which is very similar in terms of beauty. You can sit on the quiet sandy beach, enjoying the peace and quiet, and listen for the loons!

To receive more information about LINDEN LEA ON LONG LAKE, write or call: 279 South Long Lake Road, Traverse City, MI 49684 (616) 943-9182

SOURDOUGH BISCUITS (WITH STARTER)

Sourdough Starter:
1 pkg. dry yeast
2 1/2 cups warm water
2 cups sifted flour
1 tablespoon sugar
After using starter add:
3/4 cup flour
3/4 cup water
1 teaspoon sugar

Sourdough Biscuits:
1 cup sourdough starter
1/4 cup oil
1 cup flour
1/2 teaspoon salt
1/4 teaspoon soda
2 teaspoons baking powder

For starter: Dissolve yeast in 1/2 cup warm water. Stir in remainder of warm water, 2 cups flour and 1 tablespoon sugar, and beat until smooth. Cover with cheesecloth; let stand at room temperature 5 - 10 days, stirring 2 or 3 times a day. After it has stood at least 5 days, cover and refrigerate until used. After using starter, add flour, water and sugar as directed above. Stir. Let stand at room temperature until bubbly, at least one day. Refrigerate. If not used in 10 days, add 1 teaspoon sugar. Add sugar every 10 days if not used. For sourdough biscuits: Mix sourdough starter & oil. Sift together flour, salt, soda, and baking powder, add to sourdough mixture. Mix well. Knead on floured board 6 times. Roll out & cut. Bake on ungreased baking sheet at 425° - 450° for 12 - 15 minutes. Makes 8 - 10 biscuits.

LAKE TO LAKE, organized in 1983, has grown to 200 members in less than 10 years. A member directory with descriptive listings is published annually. Meeting and conferences offer opportunities for innkeepers to keep current with industry trends. The office is open daily and the director is available to answer questions, & provide reference material, or other sources of information for successful innkeeping. We work with travel writers and the MI Travel Bureau, providing "start-up" information, publication of a newsletter, and promotion of the association and its members.

To receive more information about LAKE TO LAKE B&B ASSOCIATION write or call: Jan Kerr, 7900 S. Lakeshore Dr., Cedar, MI 49621 (616) 228-7014

SWISS AND SHRIMP BAKE

- **6 slices of white bread, trimmed**
- **4 tablespoons melted butter**
- **1 cup Swiss cheese, grated**
- **2 scallions, chopped (including green tops)**
- **1/2 lb. cooked salad shrimp**
- **1/2 teaspoon salt**
- **1/2 teaspoon dijon mustard**
- **1 1/2 cups milk**
- **1/2 cup sour cream or yogurt**
- **3 eggs**

Preheat oven to 350°. Cube bread and dredge in melted butter. Arrange half the bread in an 8" baking dish. Sprinkle with half the cheese, scallions, and shrimp. Repeat with remaining bread and toppings. Beat together salt, dijon mustard, milk, sour cream/yogurt, and eggs until thoroughly combined. Pour mixture over bread layers and chill overnight. Bake covered for 30 minutes and uncovered for 10 minutes until golden brown and firm. Let set 5 - 10 minutes before serving. Makes 6 - 8 servings.

DULEY'S STATE STREET INN was built in 1898 by one of the city's wealthy lumber barons, Gustov Von Platten. The home has inspired many "firsts" throughout its history. It was the first house in town to have electricity, powered by Von Platten's own mill, which drew many visitors at dusk to gaze at the illuminated 3-story dwelling. John & Sandy Duley, the innkeepers, renovated the family residence into a Bed & Breakfast in 1989, thus establishing Boyne City's first B&B. They have been fortunate to be a part of many wonderful "firsts" too - a romantic marriage proposal, a bride and groom giggling as they sign Mr. and Mrs. for the first time, and most fondly, a child's first steps. Every guest contributes to the rewards of owning a Bed & Breakfast.

To receive more information about DULEY'S STATE STREET INN write or call: 303 State St., Boyne City, MI 49712 (616) 582-7855

DESSERTS

APPLE CRISP

8 large, tart & juicy apples
1 cup flour
1 1/2 cups sugar
1 stick butter (1/2 cup)
Cinnamon or nutmeg

Peel and slice apples into a 9" square pan. Fill pan to the top. Mix flour and sugar, cut in butter and blend. Sprinkle this mixture on top of apples, then sprinkle on cinnamon or nutmeg. Bake at 375° for about 45 minutes. Top should be crusty, and apples well-cooked. Serve with whipped cream. Makes 6 - 8 servings.

Origin: My mother.

---

435 FIFTH STREET, built in 1905, just opened as an inn in July, 1992. Guests enjoy the fireplace in the upstairs parlor and an unusual tree in the backyard.

To receive more information about 435 FIFTH STREET write or call:
435 Fifth Street, Manistee, MI 49660 (616) 723-2904

CARROT COOKIES

3/4 cup butter or margarine
3/4 cup brown sugar
1/2 cup sugar
1 egg
1 teaspoon vanilla
1 3/4 cups flour
1 teaspoon baking powder
1/4 teaspoon baking soda
1/4 teaspoon salt
1/4 teaspoon cloves
1/2 teaspoon cinnamon
2 cups rolled oats
1/2 cup raisins
1 cup finely shredded carrots

Beat butter and sugars until light and fluffy. Add egg and vanilla; beat. Sift flour, baking powder, soda, salt, cloves, and cinnamon; beat until combined. Stir in oats, raisins, and carrots. Drop by tablespoonsful on ungreased cookie sheet. Bake at 375° for 10 - 12 minutes or until edges are golden. Cool on wire rack. Makes 2 1/2 dozen large or 4 dozen regular size cookies.

THE BRILEY INN is not an old physical structure, although all rooms are filled with late 1800 or early 1900 furniture and light fixtures. Located in Briley Township, which was named after the owners' great-grandfather. Each room has a view of the Thunder Bay River, offering canoeing and fishing. Also located within minutes of 3 great golf courses.

To receive more information about THE BRILEY INN write or call:
McArthur Road, Rte. 2, Atlanta, MI 49709 (517) 785-4784

CHRISTMAS CAKE

8 oz. pkg. cream cheese
1/2 lb. butter
1 1/2 cups sugar
1 1/2 teaspoons vanilla
4 eggs
2 1/4 cups flour
1 1/2 teaspoons baking powder
1 cup candied cherries
1/2 cup chopped pecans

Thoroughly blend cream cheese, butter, sugar and vanilla. Add eggs, one at a time, mixing well. Gradually add 2 cups flour and baking powder. Combine remaining 1/4 cup flour with cherries and nuts, and fold into batter. Pour into greased 10" bundt or tube pan. Bake at 325° for 1 hour and 20 minutes. Cool 5 minutes. Remove from pan.

Origin: This delicious cake comes courtesy of Kristine's mother.

Dan, Kristine, and Gary escaped corporate life in Chicago and took over an existing inn, renaming it after Dan's Golden Retriever, Bo. One of the nicest surprises they've encountered as innkeepers has been the number of guests who become good friends. Each spring, THE RED DOG looks forward to a visit from five fantastic ladies who have gotten together every year since 1978. They had worked together at Notre Dame University, but through the years, went their separate ways. However, once a year they leave husbands, children, and jobs behind and travel from as far away as Alabama to Room 2 for their "Sacred Saugatuck Weekend." Next year, they plan to bring each of their daughters for a special 15th anniversary weekend that Saugatuck and THE RED DOG will not soon forget!

To receive more information about THE RED DOG B&B write or call:
132 Mason St., Saugatuck, MI 49453 (616) 857-8851

DELICIOUS CARAMELS

1 cup granulated sugar
1 cup dark Karo syrup
1 cup real butter
14 oz. can sweetened condensed milk
1 teaspoon vanilla

In medium saucepan mix sugar, Karo syrup and butter over medium heat. Continue stirring until mixture comes to a "ploppy" boil. Time for 7 minutes, NOT stirring. Then add condensed milk. Mix well, and continue stirring over medium heat. When mixture comes to a "ploppy" boil again, time for 13 minutes, stirring constantly. Take off heat, and add vanilla. Mix well, and pour into well-buttered 8" x 8" glass pan. Cool overnight at room temperature. Cut into bite-sized squares and wrap. Makes approximately 70 caramels.

"The Saga of Bob and Marge" is probably the most memorable story of a HARBOR HOUSE INN guest. It began the night the inn opened in 1987 and continues to this day. You must understand, Bob and Marge are fictional characters whose lives have unfolded between the covers of two of our guest books at the HARBOR HOUSE. The authors of the story are our guests who add a paragraph, or sometimes several pages to the continuing saga of this infamous couple. Bob and Marge's lives have changed a lot since that first night they stayed at the HARBOR HOUSE, but the inn remains the same - warm, cozy fireplaces in the rooms, whirlpool bathtubs, sumptuous breakfasts, and distinguished personal service.

To receive more information about HARBOR HOUSE INN write or call:
114 South Harbor Drive, Grand Haven, MI 49417
(616) 846-0610 or (800) 841-0610

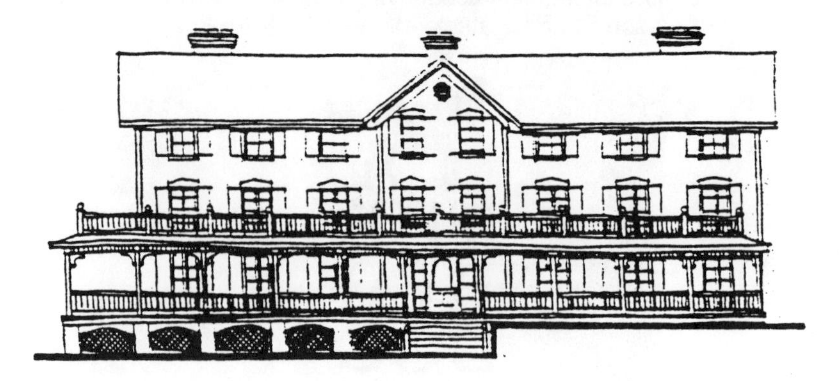

LIME CURD FOR FLORA

1 cup fresh squeezed lime juice, with pulp (about 6 limes)
1 cup sugar
1/2 cup unsalted butter, cut into pieces
1 tablespoon grated lime peel
6 fresh eggs

Cook fresh lime juice and pulp in a saucepan over medium heat, along with the sugar, butter, and lime peel, until sugar and butter have both melted. Transfer to a blender, where the eggs have been slightly beaten together. Add hot mixture a small amount at a time, so it won't cook the eggs. Blend constantly. Then return mixture to the saucepan and heat, stirring constantly, until mixture thickens. Pour into glass containers and chill. Makes 2 - 8 oz. cups.

I found my farm in 1987, and my family antiques arrived from Pennsylvania in a large van, which stopped to piggyback my mother's piano from town. Remodeling began on the houses, and the barn filled with sheep, peacocks, chickens, and cats. I had everything but knowledge of farming, and began at once to educate myself in the ways of the country woman, while following my dream to open an inn. Last June "West Virginia Flora" arrived at the inn. She was older than she looked and wore sneakers "to get around faster". Before long we were hiking together behind the creek in search of wild blackberries. Weeks later, the mailman brought 2 jars of her homemade jam. Here's one for Flora. . .

To receive more information about REYNOLDS HOUSE AT STONEFIELD FARM write or call: 5259 West Ellsworth, Ann Arbor, MI 48103 (313) 995-0301

OATMEAL PECAN DREAMS

1 cup (2 sticks) margarine
1/2 cup sugar
1 cup flour
1/2 cup oatmeal
1 1/4 teaspoons vanilla
12 pecan halves cut in half, lengthwise

With a recipe this simple, anyone can have homebaked cookies ANYtime! Put all ingredients except pecans into food processor or blender. Blend until completely mixed. Drop by teaspoonsful (or make into small balls) onto an ungreased cookie sheet. Press 1 pecan piece into each cookie. Bake at 350° for 10 - 15 minutes. Yield: 2 dozen cookies.

Origin: My mom's friend Vi gave her this recipe, back when ladies were trying to figure out things to do with their new kitchen gadget, - the blender!

THE PARK HOUSE, built in 1857, is Saugatuck's oldest residence. Originally built as both a family residence and saw mill bunk house, much of the history of Saugatuck has passed through its doorway. Innkeepers Lynda & Joe Petty have learned that a bit of the Park House seems to have a way of leaving with its guests. A recent guest told them he had been looking for the inn for 20 years! Seems as a young grad student in the '50's, he had headed out on a holiday, accidentally ending up at The Park House. Apparently much of the trip was forgotten, even the name and location, but the inn and its owner were not. In recent years, he had been trying to rediscover the inn but was unsuccessful until he happened upon a drawing of the inn in an advertisement!

To receive more information about THE PARK HOUSE write or call:
888 Holland St., Saugatuck, MI 49453 (800) 321-4535

PEACH COBBLER

- **1 1/2 sticks margarine, melted**
- **3/4 cup sugar**
- **2 cups fresh peaches, peeled and sliced**
- **3/4 cup flour**
- **1/2 teaspoon baking powder**
- **1/2 cup milk**

Melt margarine in bottom of casserole baking dish. Mix 3/4 cup sugar with peaches in separate bowl and let stand while mixing the rest of dry ingredients and milk. Add fruit and sugar mixture to casserole with melted margarine. Pour batter over fruit and bake until done at 350° approximately 1 hour.

Origin: My Texas friend who loves to cook and eat and root for the Texas Rangers, gave me this easy recipe one hot summer day.

Many guests rave about the beauty of the outdoor nature setting of our Bed & Breakfast amidst tall shade trees, bubbling spring-fed creek, and flower gardens. Catching sight of various wildlife (who also call this their home) while exploring the enchanting trail walks are high on the pleasure list. This was best summed up by an 11 year old girl from Florida who exclaimed, "This is better than Disney World!"

To receive more information about BED & BREAKFAST AT LUDINGTON write or call: 2458 S. Beaune Rd., Ludington, MI 49431 (616) 843-9768

PUMPKIN CHEESECAKE BARS

1 pkg. pound cake mix (16 oz.)
3 eggs
2 tablespoons butter or margarine, melted
8 oz. cream cheese, softened
1 can sweetened condensed milk (14 oz.)
1 can pumpkin pie filling (18 oz.)
1/2 cup chopped nuts

Preheat oven to 350°. In large mixer bowl, on low speed, combine cake mix, 1 egg and melted margarine until crumbly. Press onto bottom of 15" x 10" x 1" jellyroll pan. Set aside. In larger mixer bowl, beat cream cheese until smooth. Gradually beat in sweetened condensed milk, 2 eggs, and pumpkin, mix well. Pour over crust, sprinkle nuts on top. Bake for 30 - 35 minutes or until set. Cool. Chill, cut into bars. Store in refrigerator. Makes 48 bars.

THE BAYSIDE INN is the perfect lodging choice on the water for all exciting year round events in Saugatuck. Located footsteps from downtown restaurants and shops, and close to marinas, beaches, and nature trails. Once a charming boathouse, now an elegant and contemporary waterfront B&B featuring a central spacious living area with cozy fireplace and romantic view of the water. Each room has private bath and deck. VCR's are available. Perfect for group gatherings and mini-conventions. When the current owners purchased it, the property was falling down and condemned. Now it is restored, with dormer roof for a spectacular river view.

To receive more information about BAYSIDE INN write or call:
618 Water St., P.O. Box 1001, Saugatuck, MI 49453
(616) 857-4321

RICE PUDDING

2 cups milk
3/4 cup rice
1/2 cup raisins
1/4 cup butter
3 beaten eggs
2 cups half & half
1/2 cup sugar
1 teaspoon vanilla
1/2 teaspoon salt
1/2 teaspoon cinnamon
1/4 teaspoon nutmeg

In heavy saucepan, bring 2 cups milk, uncooked rice, and raisins to boil. Reduce heat, cover, and cook over very low heat about 15 minutes. Remove from heat, stir in butter. In bowl stir together eggs, half & half, sugar, vanilla, and salt. Stir rice mixture into egg mixture. Pour into baking dish. Bake in 325° oven for 30 minutes. Stir well, adding the cinnamon and nutmeg. Bake for 15 - 20 minutes more or until knife inserted in center comes out clean. Serve warm or chilled. Makes 6 servings.

DEWEY LAKE MANOR is a century-old house sitting atop a knoll overlooking picturesque Dewey Lake, in the Irish Hills of southern Michigan. It was built by A. F. Dewey, "a prosperous farmer of the area," who owned the lake and all the land around it. It is a quiet, peaceful place to enjoy the sweet sounds of the summer nights or the quiet stillness of the frozen lake. A recent guest from Pittsburgh came into the house after an early morning walk by the lake, with a tranquil, slightly bemused look on his face. "I've just been listening to the sounds out there, it's wonderful." Summer in the country truly is wonderful.

To receive more information about DEWEY LAKE MANOR B&B write or call: 11811 Laird Rd., Brooklyn, MI 49230 (517) 467-7122

SAM HILL CAKE

1/4 cup butter or margarine
1/3 cup sugar
2 eggs
1/2 cup milk
3/4 cup flour
1 teaspoon grated lemon peel
Graham cracker crumbs

Topping:
2 cups sour cream
1/3 cup sugar

Fresh sliced strawberries for garnish

Butter a tart pan or an 8" cake pan. Sprinkle with graham cracker crumbs. Cream butter and sugar. Beat in eggs one at a time. Add milk, flour, and lemon peel and blend well. Pour into pan and bake at 350° for about 10 minutes. Turn cake out onto serving plate and cool. Mix sugar with sour cream and fill center of the tart. Arrange strawberries (or other fruit of your choice) in a pleasing pattern. Serve chilled.

Origin: Sam Hill lived in Marshall.

Our guests often call to tell us they are coming, and would love for us to make a certain treat which we bake!

To receive more information about NATIONAL HOUSE INN write or call: 102 S. Parkview, Marshall, MI 49068 (616) 781-7374

SHARON'S APPLE CAKE

4 cups apples, diced (no need to peel)
2 cups sugar
2 eggs
2/3 cup oil
2 teaspoons vanilla
2 cups flour
1 1/2 teaspoons baking soda
1 teaspoon salt
1 teaspoon cinnamon
1 cup chopped nuts

Mix diced apples and sugar and let set until apples juice. Beat eggs. Add oil and vanilla, and mix. Add flour, baking soda, salt, and cinnamon and mix until blended. Add apple mixture and nuts. Mix just until combined. Bake in 9" x 13" pan or bundt pan. Bake at 350° for 50 - 60 minutes.

THE PEBBLE HOUSE was built in 1912 by two couples from Chicago, who later built 60 summer cottages surrounding their lakeside residence. The Craftsman style house is constructed of decorative block, small stones, and wood. Gate and fenceposts are also of the stones, which give the inn it's name. Arts & crafts furnishings welcome guests back to a simpler, more comfortable era. A man in his forties who had summered in one of the cottages as a child, was so overwhelmed by memories as he toured the inn, that in a tiny voice he asked, "Could you possibly make me a cup of cocoa - with marshmallows?" I did. Today's inn incorporates two of the original cottages, the main house, a tennis court, rustically furnished screen house, and Lake Michigan beach access.

To receive more information about THE PEBBLE HOUSE write or call: 15093 Lakeshore Rd., Lakeside, MI 49116 (616) 469-1416

SUGAR COOKIES

- 1 cup butter or margarine, softened
- 1/2 cup sugar
- 1 large egg
- 1 tablespoon vanilla
- 1/4 teaspoon salt
- 2 cups flour
- Pink or red colored sugar

Heat oven to 325°. In medium bowl, with electric mixer, beat butter, sugar, egg, vanilla, and salt, until fluffy. Beat in flour. Refrigerate dough, tightly wrapped, at least 1 hour. Roll out dough to 1/4" thickness. Cut with heart-shaped cookie cutter. Place cookies, 1/2" apart, on ungreased baking sheets. Sprinkle with colored sugar. Bake cookies 12 - 15 minutes or until edges just start to brown. Makes 3 dozen 2 1/2" hearts.

Origin: From working with Girl Scouts. It's so simple!

FRIEDA'S BED & BREAKFAST is owned by Frieda Putnam, a Ukraine native, who opened her home to 18 year old Anya Peregoud, a Soviet cancer patient and her mother, Tanya. Frieda interpreted for the Peregouds for the press and public, when they spoke about Chernobyl and the devastating effects it has had on Anya. She has lost a leg to cancer, and also has cancerous nodes in her lungs. She hopes to return home to Crimea, 350 miles south of Chernobyl when her treatment in the United States is complete. She has a 50% chance of cancer recovery.

To receive more information about FRIEDA'S B&B write or call:
13141 Omena Point Road, Omena, MI 49674 (616) 386-7274

SUPREME BANANA DESSERT

1/2 cup sour cream
2 tablespoons sugar
2 tablespoons orange juice
1 teaspoon orange peel
2 large bananas
Granola for topping

Mix sour cream, sugar, orange juice, and orange peel together. Slice up bananas. Drop bananas into mixture. Sprinkle granola over top. Makes 2 servings. You can double or triple recipe as required. Also great for breakfast.

Guests from all over the world have stayed at our inn, but I will never forget one special person. A businessman from Florida came to stay with us. As we were visiting in the common room, he kept looking around the room. I asked him if something was wrong. He said, no, it was just that he and his wife had almost bought our bed and breakfast just before we had purchased the property. As we came to find out, he was a plant manager of a company in our town, and had been transferred to the plant in Florida. What a surprise for us!

To receive more information about BRIAROAKS B&B, write or call:
2980 N. Adrian Hwy., Adrian, MI 49221 (517) 263-1659

HOUSEHOLD HINTS FROM THE INNKEEPERS

When storing linens in your linen closet, place both sheets and one pillowcase inside the other pillowcase. Place on shelf. Looks good, and very handy for cleaning person - no searching for lost cases, etc.

Torch Lake B&B

Instead of leaving chocolates on guests' pillows, leave a fresh bowl of popcorn in their rooms after they leave for the evening. I get rave reviews for this touch.

Torch Lake B&B

In rooms where smoking is allowed, place an open dish of white vinegar. It helps absorb the smoke smell.

Saravilla B&B

Mix up double batches of muffin batter and store in the refrigerator until time to bake (up to 3 - 4 weeks).

Stonehedge Inn B&B

Overripe bananas can be frozen in their skins, then thawed before use. Cut off the top of banana and down the side with shears. Squeeze into a cup.

Stonehedge Inn B&B

To remove water stains from glassware and crystal, especially those which are left in flower vases, soak in dry dishwasher detergent and water.

Bellaire B&B

Use a paper towel to wash down the bathroom. Do the toilet last and flush the paper towel away with the dirt!

Bellaire B&B

We have a baby monitor in the hallway upstairs - it gives us the security of knowing everything is okay - with guests and our daughters.

Bellaire B&B

To remove cigarette smoke odor from a room, place a few dryer sheets on carpet or furniture and close the room for a day. Dryer sheets soak up the odor and leave a fresh scent!

American Inn

Make your own napkin rings from creative twist paper. They can be shaped into bows or animal shapes. Available in enough colors to coordinate with any table setting!

Essenmacher's B&B

Place about 1/4 cup white vinegar in the sink with your detergent for extra sparkle of china, crystal and silver.

House on the Hill

Many recipes call for buttermilk. For quick buttermilk for those morning muffins, use 1 tablespoon lemon juice to 1 cup milk. Let set for 10 minutes.

Hidden Pond B&B

Keep an old toothbrush in your cleaning caddy to scrub the edges around faucets with Fantastik spray.

The Kingsley House

Use your old face cloths and hand towels for cleaning rags.

The Kingsley House

Have a puzzle available for guests to enjoy after a day out on the town. It promotes a homey atmosphere, and is an easy way of entertainment.

The Kingsley House

Keep amenities baskets in each room with extra soap, facecloths, shampoo, toilet paper and Kleenex. Put extra towels and blankets in dresser drawer, so guests will not be short of supplies.

The Kingsley House

Add a jar of mints by the bedside to keep everyone happy with fresh-smelling breath.

The Kingsley House

We buy gallon jugs of car windshield cleaner from K-Mart, to use as glass cleaner. Works great, and it's very cheap!

Heritage House B&B

I dry throw rugs on our big hammock outdoors.

Heritage House B&B

When you have sheets that need to be ironed, iron them on the bed, right after they have been washed.

Boyden House Inn B&B

Use fragrant herb leaves from the garden, such as lemon balm, mint, or lavender, to enhance fresh flower room arrangements.

Fountain Hill B&B

Accumulate stale rolls and bread in a plastic bag in the freezer, and sometime when using the blender or food processor, grate them for fine "fresh" bread crumbs. Place back in freezer for a constant supply, always available.

Heald-Lear House

Add a slice of lemon to ice water for an elegant touch.

Mary Helen Phillips

Keep up with health-conscious guests who sincerely watch their fat intake. Reduce fat in recipes by substituting ricotta cheese for cream cheese, and by substituting natural applesauce for oil, margarine or shortening in muffins and cakes. Use nonfat or lowfat yogurt for sour cream.

Dutch Colonial Inn

Use Pledge on a feather duster when cleaning mini blinds. The dust will not stick to blinds and cleaning is kept to a minimum.

Stevens Whitehouse on the Lake

To keep fiberglass showers and tubs gleaming, use "Gel-Gloss" which produces a high lustre and elminates water spotting and surface stains. It is found at lumber yards and hardware stores.

Chaffin's Balmoral Farm

To hard cook eggs, prick large end with a needle to prevent eggs from cracking.

Chaffin's Balmoral Farm

Remove kitchenware labels with water and cooking oil. Fill pot, pan or jar with hot water to loosen label so most of it can be removed, then apply oil to rub off remaining paper and adhesive.

Summit Place B&B

Use the plastic mesh bags that hold onions to scour pans. They fold easily into pads, and can be unfolded to rinse clean.

Summit Place B&B

Add an orange peel to the tea pot a few minutes before tea is served for delicious flavor.

Summit Place B&B

To clean chrome, wipe with rubbing alcohol on a soft cloth.

Manitou Manor B&B

Put a piece of bread in with your brown sugar to keep it soft.

Manitou Manor B&B

To remove laundry stains mix together equal parts of Dawn dishwashing detergent, ammonia, and water. Pour on stain, wait a few minutes, then wash as usual.

Manitou Manor B&B

Ball point ink marks on clothing will easily be removed by first spraying with hair spray, followed by hand rubbing with warm water and laundry detergent. Then put in washing machine with regular laundry.

Bed & Breakfast at Ludington

For no streak windows and mirrors, use 1 cup vinegar and 1 cup alcohol to 1 quart water. Wash with a soft cloth, and wipe dry with paper towel. Stand back and admire! "Let the sun shine in!"

Doll House Inn

If you have problems keeping your ferns alive, try this: Cut the fern at the base of the plant, about 6 inches above the soil. Place outside in the summer and by fall you will have a "new" fern growing. May need to be repeated a few times for a fuller fern.

The Ludington House B&B

When boiling fresh Michigan corn, add sugar to the water instead of salt. Salt will toughen the corn.

435 Fifth Street

Use Polident to clean flower vases. It removes a lot of the residue which builds up in vases.

Huron House B&B

Never mix anything with bleach.

Bear River Valley B&B

Wash windows with a mild solution of ammonia and warm water. Use a hand mop and squeegee like professional window cleaners.

Paint Creek B&B

Keep a spray bottle with diluted bleach. It removes mildew around shower floors quickly.

Village Rose B&B

For dishwasher film on dishes: Add Barkeepers Friend to your regular washing cycle.

Beechwood Manor B&B

For problems with hair that collects in the bathroom, wind a strip of wide masking tape around your hand, and "dust" everything, including the floor. Then proceed to clean as usual.

Rummel's Tree Haven

Use 1 cap full of Avon soft pink bubble bath in 1 gallon water to wash your car. Leaves it shining clean.

Seascape B&B

Have a problem with onions spoiling? Take an old pair of panty hose, drop an onion down in the foot and knot it off. Then drop another onion, and tie a knot. Do this until both legs are full. Hang by the waist. Cut the onion off below knot as needed.

Seascape B&B

For fluffier omelets, add a pinch of cornstarch before beating.

Seascape B&B

Soft Scrub with Bleach takes stains out of white linens and towels. Test a spot first. Do not get it on colors.

A Country Place B&B

Difficult stains on pillow cases may be removed before washing by making a paste of baking soda. Slather it on the stain and let it set overnight before washing.

Ross House

When doing laundry, hydrogen peroxide will take out blood stains.

Cider House B&B

Place a board near the front door with all the guests' names. As they come in for the night, have them cross off their name. The last couple locks the door and turns off the lights.

Cider House B&B

Cut an old shower curtain with pinking shears and make it into an apron. Attach ties at the top and the middle and wear it when doing messy indoor or outdoor jobs.

The Victoriana 1898

Use Lestoil to remove coffee, lipstick, and chocolate stains from linens.

The Victoriana 1898

Vacuum the bathroom floor before washing it to halve cleaning time.

Heather House

When stripping bedrooms and bathrooms of their dirty linens and towels, check for spots or stains and rub the area with a spot remover stick. If it is a very bad stain, tie the stained article in a knot, so you can find it easier in the laundry room to work on it further.

Timekeeper's Inn

Put muffin batter in tins lined with paper cups and freeze. In the morning take out as many as needed, 30 minutes before baking, to thaw. Bake as directed. Have the lovely aroma of fresh baked muffins, eliminate the rush in the morning, and no waste.

Cherry Knoll Farm B&B

Personalize small individual soaps by putting small address stickers on them. If the label is in fancy script, the end result looks classy.

Bed & Breakfast at The Pines

Have all ingredients measured out the night before for muffins or other baked goods. No fuss in the morning, just mix, bake and serve!

Bed & Breakfast at The Pines

Salt and vinegar or lemon juice clean copper beautifully.

South Cliff Inn

If your refrigerator is on the port side, don't open it when the ship is healing over toward starboard.

The Tall Ship Malabar

Mix together equal portions of flour and shortening to grease muffin tins. This can be kept indefinitely and is a quick way to prevent sticking and burning.

The Gingerbread House

The BEST way to clean a ceramic tile kitchen floor: Dip a large terry cloth rag in vinegar and water. Squeeze out water. Drop the rag on the floor, and using your foot, scrub the floor clean. Rinse rag and repeat as needed. The floor will shine and your knees won't hurt!

The Pebble House

To remove the rubber marks your vacuum cleaner might leave on dark furniture legs: Rub gently with rubbing alcohol, follow with furniture polish.

Country Inn of Grand Blanc

For holiday cookie baking timesaver: Drop dough onto a tray. Freeze until firm. Put in moisture-proof bags. Store up to 6 months. Thaw at room temperature, and bake as recipe states.

Ellsworth House

When cleaning plain walls and ceilings, use a floor mop. An O'Cedar mop that can be squeezed out is a good choice.

Marina Guest House

Keep your ice cubes in a brown paper bag in the freezer and they stay separated and easy to use.

The Park House

Buy a small spiral notebook to help keep your decorating organized. For each room in the house, staple in wallpaper samples and paint chips from the paint store. Your colors are always available when shopping, or for buying new paint 5 years down the line.

The Park House

A bottle of mineral spirits removes tough ink stains and other hard to get out spots without damaging the fabric. It is inexpensive and can be purchased at a hardware store.

Jan Kerr

To remove hair cream or make-up from pillowcases, place a little stain remover and water in a glass bowl. Then add the pillowcase, pop it into the microwave, and bring to a boil.

Jan Kerr

INDEX OF BED & BREAKFASTS

NOTES

NOTES

NOTES

NOTES

NOTES

NOTES

NOTES

NOTES

NOTES

ORDER FORMS

Just Inn Time For Breakfast

I would like to order *Just Inn Time For Breakfast, A Cookbook From The Michigan Lake To Lake Bed and Breakfast Association.* I have indicated the quantity below. MAIL THIS ORDER TO: Winters Publishing, P.O. Box 501, Greensburg, IN 47240.

_____ *Just Inn Time For Breakfast* $10.95 each ___________

Shipping Charge $2.00 each ___________

Sales Tax (Indiana residents ONLY) $ .65 each ___________

TOTAL ___________

Please send to:

Name: ____

Address: ____

City: ____________________ State: ____________ Zip: ____________

Just Inn Time For Breakfast

I would like to order *Just Inn Time For Breakfast, A Cookbook From The Michigan Lake To Lake Bed and Breakfast Association.* I have indicated the quantity below. MAIL THIS ORDER TO: Winters Publishing, P.O. Box 501, Greensburg, IN 47240.

_____ *Just Inn Time For Breakfast* $10.95 each ___________

Shipping Charge $2.00 each ___________

Sales Tax (Indiana residents ONLY) $ .65 each ___________

TOTAL ___________

Please send to:

Name: ____

Address: ____

City: ____________________ State: ____________ Zip: ____________
